Investing Better Than A Money Manager
The Rise Of Retail Investing

Trent Welsh
MBA, B.A. Psychology

Cover Design By
Sarah Welsh

For Sarah, Alexander, Elizabeth, Lilian, Maximus, and Constantine

Contents

Chapter 1 The Time Value of Money

Chapter 2 Your IRA

Chapter 3 Your 401k

Chapter 4 Being Diversified

Chapter 5 Mutual Funds

Chapter 6 Index Funds

Chapter 7 Preparing For Single Stock Risk

Chapter 8 The Information Technology Sector

Chapter 9 The Financial Sector

Chapter 10 The Health Care Sector

Chapter 11 The Communications Services Sector

Chapter 12 The Materials Sector

Chapter 13 The Consumer Discretionary Sector

Chapter 14 The Energy Sector

Chapter 15 The Consumer Staples Sector

Chapter 16 The Industrials Sector

Chapter 17 The Utilities Sector

Chapter 18 The Real Estate Sector

Chapter 19 Bonds

Chapter 20 Domestic Vs International

Chapter 21 Bitcoin And Cryptocurrencies

Chapter 22 Over-The-Counter Trading

Chapter 23 Multiple Ticker Symbols

Chapter 24 Treasuries

Chapter 25 Portfolio Examples

Index of Terms

Chapter 1
The Time Value of Money

What Goes Down Must Come Up, At Least For The Stock Market.
- Author

"What's Hoover Got To Do With It? Besides, I Had A Better Year Than He Did."
- Babe Ruth

    Nothing is more important to the average investor than taking advantage of the time value of money over the course of your life as it winds continuously towards retirement. Over the last 100+ years, markets have formed an upward sloping line, which means that the earlier you start investing, the more money you should logically expect to have when you reach retirement age. Although down, or bear, markets can go on for years, or even decades, each and every one in history has ultimately been a buying opportunity as the market continues to climb steadily higher over time.

    Here is how the stock market has fared from 1896 up to 2018 with a steady predictable rise. Even the Great Depression looks like a normal regular pullback instead of a world-ending event that many people thought it was at the time as in this time frame it is a barely discernable blip.

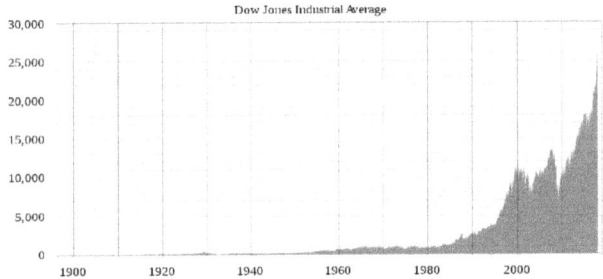

Not only have markets appreciate dramatically in value over time, that action appears to be accelerating. By looking at the simple charts above, chart action appears to be speeding up with higher highs and lower lows as the market runs hotter and hotter. The point is, it's very hard to be a loser in the general market over an extended period of time. Also, the longer you are in the game, the greater the rewards for playing the game ultimately should be. Of course, this theory only works until it doesn't work, but I'll bet my money on the stock market appreciating over the next 30 years rather than shorting it or holding onto cash. Life is too short to not make common sense bets on your future.

Now, here is a mathematical formula used to calculate the future value of money by inputting the interest rate you expect to receive over the number of years you expect to be investing over.

$$FV = PV(1 + i)^n$$

FV = Future Value
PV = Present Value
i = Interest Rate
n = Number of Years

Not exactly the most interesting thing to most people, but notice the fact that the main variables that determine the future value of money in this model are the interest rate that you receive on your money over time, and the number of years that are involved. The exponent n does nothing to affect the number 1 in the equation until you add in the interest rate variable i. 1

to whatever exponent for the number of years n is always equal to 1, but by adding in the interest part of the equation, even small differences in interest rates can end up making a significant difference in the future value of your money, as those small differences are magnified exponentially by the number of years n that you invest.

Invest early, invest often, and invest over the long-term, and the odds will favor you in achieving significant gains in your retirement savings over the course of your adult life.

This also means that market "crashes", "recessions", "depressions", "corrections", and "meltdowns" are ultimately buying opportunities for long-term players. I try to opportunistically invest money into my IRA at the beginning of each year regardless of how the market fared in the previous year. If an investor could predict market cycles, and market ups and downs, then they would have no need to read books any more or plan as knowing what will happen beforehand would mean they could make maximum opportunistic bets and own a Hawaiian island with minimal effort and time. Unfortunately, no investor or machine can predict what the market will do tomorrow so it is ultimately a grind to get to the top of the retirement mountain.

The best most investors can do is make a prediction based on momentum (we have been up 5 days straight, so I'm guessing tomorrow will be up also), or based on a return to the mean prediction (today the market rocketed up 5% so I predict that tomorrow the market most likely be a down day for the market to get back towards normality). Instead of spending tons of time looking at charts and numbers, I prefer to look for long-term gains with solid enduring companies that will make up my retirement portfolio years from now.

Chapter 2
IRA's

To Later Conquer The World, First Conquer Yourself.
- Author

"Veni, Vidi, Vici."
- Caesar

The best way to start investing is by putting some money into an IRA, either at the beginning of a calendar year, or with a monthly donation. The advantage of compounding money and returns over time means that starting as early as possible (18-25 years old) will mean a potential big difference on the balance of your retirement portfolio when it comes time to start drawing the funds.

One of the biggest concerns with IRA's is just starting the process. Taking that first step is crucial, and figuring out what type of account you want to start to get the ball rolling. You can set up an account through a broker, such as Edward Jones, whom you can meet with once a year to discuss portfolio strategies and rebalancing. Basically, this includes determining how much money you want to have saved by retirement, and how much you realistically need to save yearly to reach your goals. They can also advise you on how to set up your initial portfolio mixture and balancing for how much risk you want to take to achieve your investment goals.

Another option that is easier than many may know is by setting up a self-directed IRA through a broker like Charles Schwab. This process is pretty quick and easy and allows the investor to actively trade their IRA account using a regular computer, or even by using a basic smart-phone and the brokerages latest trading app. Either way is ultimately fine, it mostly depends on how much you want to pay others to maintain and rebalance your account, or if you want to take the initiative and personal responsibility for building and managing your own retirement portfolio through actively trading yourself.

I personally started out with Edward Jones because that is what my family was familiar with, so I had an agent that I could indirectly relate to means they had dealt with other family members in the past. I started out with a Roth IRA, which seemed like a more intelligent choice to me at the time, means I had a simple job and simple money. I was much more into paying potential taxes now so that the money would grow tax free over time and into retirement instead of taxes later as with a Traditional IRA. I started with simple deposits, usually once a year, though nowhere near the maximum of $5500 a year, which was out of my ballpark back then. My agent used the funds to invest in simple globally growth based mutual funds that basically bet on the world as a whole doing better over time, which sounded great to me at the time as I believed even then that the stock market was ultimately an upward trending entity.

No matter if you start with like a $500-$1000 a year IRA donation at the beginning of the year, or do a monthly $100 donation, the key is to start the process and to get the ball moving. You should not be looking to becoming an instant millionaire at this point, but in simply setting up a nice base of mutual and index funds. This base of core holdings should help give you a solid start of diversified exposure before moving on to more specific sector or industry related stocks or bonds.

I personally think that building a $10,000 ($20,000 if married) mutual fund or broad based index fund is a great way to start. Monitoring this base will allow you to get familiar with general market moves, and the ups and downs of market runs or corrections. It is also valuable to start to see how your investments work over time in how they receive dividends or distributions over the course of the year, and to see the end of the year performance of your mutual or index fund compared to how the Dow Jones Industrial Average (DJIA) or the S&P 500 did. This is also a good time to look and see how the fees that your broker charges affects your holdings over the year, and to figure out if you are ultimately happy with your brokerage company, or if switching to a different approach would work best for you. Better to get these things figured out early on so that you can spend the most time possible investing the way that makes the most sense to you.

As you get older and your income levels hopefully increase, you might have an issue with the income restriction on Roth IRA's which might start to affect you if you make over $100k a year as a single or around $200k as a married couple. Laws are always subject to change, and dollar amounts depend on other variables and adjustments, but just be aware that once you get around those income levels, IRA contributions might become a little more complex as Roth IRA's might not be an option any more.

In my family's case, once we started reaching those income restrictions, we started having our

Edward Jones broker initially do our deposits into a Traditional IRA, then rollover the amount directly into a Roth IRA for our regular donation. This loophole, if done right away, means that you have no gains or losses to report for your Traditional IRA that would have tax implications, but you still get the benefits of tax free growth in the IRA account by having it transferred into a Roth IRA account. Taxes and IRS issues tend to get more complex the older you get, and also the more money you make, so figuring out your wants and desires early on helps you in the long run.

    As I have grown older, I decided to move away from Edward Jones as my family's IRA provider by setting up my own self-directed IRA account using Charles Schwab as my broker. This coincided with Edward Jones's move to reconfigure its business model by changing how investors could use and pay for their services, which I was not as much into as I grew older and was wanting to do more individual investing. I decided to let my original Roth IRA accounts with Edward Jones continue to stand as grandfathered accounts, and instead decided to start up my own self-directed IRA account with Charles Schwab as a Traditional IRA account. I did it this way so that I wouldn't have to deal with the hassle of converting it to a Roth IRA. I am also a big fan of diversity, so I figured having some investments in a Roth IRA, and some funds in a Traditional IRA, might not be the worst thing once I reach retirement. Owning a Traditional IRA means that I don't deal with the taxes on the account now, but later on retirement instead when the funds are being withdrawn.

In today's age, I have no idea ultimately at retirement if I will be making more or less money than I do now, nor do I have any idea how tax laws will change over these years, or even what the retirement age restrictions will be when I get old enough to consider withdrawal actions. Laws change, situations change, and I am a firm believer in spreading out your risk and your assets so that you are not locked into one investment in case the world changes right before you plan to retire.

Chapter 3
401k's

Both Success And Failure Are Fleeting, Learn And Move On.
- Author

"I Have No Use For Bodyguards, But I Have Very Specific Use For Two Highly Trained Certified Public Accountants."
- Elvis Presley

As you enter into the workforce, hopefully you will have access to a 401k retirement plan, or a similar retirement benefit plan like a pension funded mostly by your employer. A lot of companies set up these tax advantaged accounts for their employees retirement with funds that match what employees provide from their paychecks, or add funds directly into a retirement account over the course of the year based on the company's earnings.

These accounts can easily take precedence over your IRA if your employer has a matching program in place. This can effectively double your investment every time you make a qualifying contribution from your paycheck. Free matching and being tax advantaged are a couple of powerful tools for your retirement portfolio, so take advantage of it as often as you possibly can.

Find out what possible investments your 401k or other retirement plan allows you to invest in, and actively coordinate it with your IRA to diversify your investments. Some company retirement plans have focuses on the company's own stock, or they can offer investments in mutual funds or index funds that fall in a broker's range of offered products set up specifically for your company. Other plans will offer you access to virtually any market product and let the employee make the investment decisions with guidance or direction from the company if you desire it.

In my case, I started out with an IRA early on, which was through Edward Jones, who charged a hefty commission on trades to go along with very much appreciated financial planning advice to get me started on the road to financial independence. I ended up setting this account to initially focus on investing in mutual funds for global growth companies, bonds, and emerging markets exposure with a diverse group of about 6 funds. After these initial investments I spent several years building a core base of mutual funds with small yearly donations while I did part-time jobs and continued to progress through college programs.

Being busy with school and life meant that I did not have the time to try and pick out individual stocks so it was easy and convenient to build up my base well past $10,000 with some yearly rebalancing if necessary after talking with my advisor. It wasn't until school for my family was completely over that I started to consider diversifying my retirement portfolio with individual stock picks in my IRA to start getting a feel for how these instruments worked. This allowed me to get a good base of knowledge as my family progressed to a company 401k plan that became the new focus of my investment path.

My family's 401k was set up with direct deposits by our employer into a Charles Schwab retirement account. I had free access to trade in virtually any investment that I wanted too that was currently offered on the market. This included mutual funds, index funds, single stocks, bonds, and even over-the-counter stocks that most regular working class people don't usually even consider in their investment decisions as opportunities. This account had simple trading fees associated with it that made it a much easier account to trade into and out of single stocks compared to my Edward Jones's account. Using Charles Schwab meant that I had access to the company's trading app designed for my smartphone, which made trading quick and easy as news filtered in throughout the day, or random ideas for trades sprang up after consideration of whatever was currently happening in the market. I love the ability to make a couple quick trades at the gym or while taking the kids out on an outing without having to set up an appointment with an advisor or leaving a message on an answering phone.

    Schwab's ease of use, and low trading fees, allowed me to set up that account focused on single stock picks across all of the market sectors that I could quickly and easily trade into and out of. This account was started after years of building a base of mutual funds at Edward Jones with my wife, before and after college, well beyond the $10,000 that I would advise most people to start with. Having a core base of non-trading investments, besides yearly potential rebalancing in mutual funds which is fee free, in an Edward Jones's account and my single stock trading picks in another Charles Schwab account helped me to keep things separate and to measure performance of my general investments against one another. This has made investing a lot more fun for me means at the end of each year I can compare my overall performance with that of the Dow Jones or S&P 500. I can also see how a more conservative Edward Jones account performs against a riskier Charles Schwab account of stocks I love for more for core long-term holdings as well as short-term bets based on how the market is trending, political changes, upcoming FDA meetings, or whatever M&A activity is in the news during that particular time of year.

Figure out what retirement benefits your employer offers and take the time to figure out how to best maximize your potential yearly savings. There is nothing like free or matching contributions so make sure you take every penny of it you can and invest it in the wisest way possible.

Chapter 4
Being Diversified

There Are Opportunities For Outsized Gains In Stocks In Every Sector At All Times. Therefore, Never Rely On One Sector To Drive All Of Your Performance.
- Author

"Let No Feeling Of Discouragement Prey Upon You, And In The End You Are Sure To Succeed."
- Abraham Lincoln

One of the main goals of investing over the years is achieving diversification and continuing to stay diversified as your retirement grows over time. This can be accomplished by starting your base core holdings with general mutual and index funds that encompass broad areas of the market not only domestically, but also internationally. When you are young, you shouldn't need that much exposure to bonds, especially if rates continue to be low compared to historical averages. However, a small percentage of your portfolio is never a bad thing as your bond exposure should grow slowly over time as you get closer to retirement, even if it is still a small percentage of your portfolio at retirement.

By intelligently spreading your capital across asset classes and sectors, you can eliminate a lot of the risk associated with any one asset or class. It would not have been a great idea to have all of your retirement money in bank stocks right before the Financial Crisis, or to have had all of your money invested in real estate right before the housing market crashed.

A diversified portfolio should have less variance (ups and downs) in it than the weighted average variance of the individual assets that make up the portfolio. Its variance as a whole should be closer to the least volatile asset in your portfolio instead of closer to the investments with higher Beta's or volatility scores. Your diversified portfolio will have some protection against major swings to the upside, and the retirement ending downside, that can bring disaster to people who have all their retirement nest eggs invested primarily in their company's own stock, like many Enron employees had before that company's implosion.

Being diversified means that you have a solid core of assets that should be able to hold up through recessions, depressions, and crashes and come out safely on the other side, even though there might be a couple company casualties along the way. This core haven of strength will also allow you to take a risky "shot" each year, if you wanted to, on a high risk asset (large volatility or Beta) such as Bitcoin, or a low market cap biotech company for example that has huge upside potential, but could also just as easily go to near 0 if clinical trial data fails to show significance for any of its candidates. These shots can make a huge difference in your portfolio each year if they hit, yet they won't kill your year if they are a small part of a diversified portfolio.

Chapter 5
Mutual Funds

Some Of The Best Stocks To Capture A Kid's Interest Include Disney, Hasbro, And Nike.
- Author

"For Fools Rush In Where Angels Fear To Tread."
- Alexander Pope

When I put in my first dollars into my IRA at Edward Jones, the money went into mutual funds. These are funds set up by different companies that consist of a wide range of stocks in the area of interest for the mutual fund. In my case, Edward Jones used American Funds as its main group of funds from which to choose from for my initial investments. Other brokers might pick from Vanguard Funds or a host of other funds that individual brokers might choose to push. If you are going the self-directed way, I'd focus on doing some good searches using your broker's software, or do some looking at great sites like Morningstar. Many sites will allow investors to check out the fees associated with each fund, and to also take a look at the fund's top holdings to make sure they align with what you are truly wanting.

The mutual funds I have used now, and in the past, in my family's IRA include American Funds EuroPacific Growth fund (AEPGX), American Funds Capital World Growth and Income fund (CWGIX), American Funds The Bond Fund of America (ABNDX), American Funds SMALLCAP World Fund (SMCWX), and American Funds New World Fund (NEWFX). Most of these funds were picked to benefit directly from global growth with both domestic and international exposure. Allocations and a couple funds have changed over time with some minor rebalancing, mainly to help compliment my other asset holdings, with the main planned changes over time most likely being a slowly growing bond fund as a percentage of my portfolio.

Here is a look at some of the main holdings of my EuroPacific Growth fund (AEPGX) as it obviously should be investing in stocks of bigger companies that correspond to the title of the fund.

EuroPacific Growth Fund Top Holdings	% of Net Assets
Samsung Electronics Co. Ltd.	3.25%
AIA Group Ltd.	2.62%
British American Tobacco PLC	2.54%
Taiwan Semiconductor Manufacturing Co. Ltd.	2.04%

Table by Trent Welsh

As you can see from the table, quite a few of mutual funds have main holdings around the 2-3% range and hold about 30-50 individual stocks in the fund. These funds will possibly do monthly, quarterly, or even yearly rebalancing to align the holdings to what the fund's prospectus goals are. So if one company has an amazing year while another has a poor year, the fund would sell the winner to buy more of the loser to get the %'s of each owned stock closer to the goals the fund originally had set up.

Most mutual funds provide investors distributions over the course of the year based on the dividends and distributions they receive from the assets they hold along with any capital appreciation returns that they are obliged to return. Every fund is set up differently, so these distributions might come monthly, quarterly, semi-annually, or annually depending on the fund prospectus.

I set up my IRA with Edward Jones with the intent of not using it as a trading account, except when I did my regular deposits, and an occasional rebalancing if it felt warranted. For this reason, I chose to have my distributions reinvested directly back into the mutual fund that gave the distribution to take advantage of compounding of the assets over time. Because the distributions get converted right back into more shares of the mutual fund, every year the number of shares I have of each fund increases on its own. This is one reason why the younger you start investing, the better your returns are likely to be by the time you decide to retire. Companies like Edward Jones also allow the purchase of partial shares of stocks, which is nice, especially with dividend reinvestment plans. So even if my monthly distribution was $5 for a bond fund, Edward Jones was still able to buy me $1/10^{th}$ of a share of the bond fund if each share was valued at $50 at the time of the distribution into my account. The ability to grow your holdings gradually over time by small amounts, and in fractional shares, adds up significantly over time. This reinvestment policy made investing more fun for me because at the end of the year, when I do my final figures and comparisons against previous years, its like an additional Christmas present seeing how many new shares I now had in my different funds over the past year without putting any additional money into those funds.

    A lot of my funds were also set up for big bonus distributions at the end of each year, as lots of funds are set up to return most of their asset growth from the past year back to investors right before the end of the year in December. So, some of my funds for example would give me approximately $50 a quarter for the first three quarters of the year then a nice $500 distribution at the end of the year based on the dividends and distributions the fund made over the last quarter along with the capital appreciation of the fund over the course of the year, which also had to be returned to shareholders based on the fund's prospectus.

    I find it very entertaining to count up my distributions and dividends from all of my holdings each and every year to directly compare to previous years as I try to grow that income every year I get older. The ultimate goal is for dividends and distributions to hopefully be a main component of my family's retirement income, and the higher those dividends and distributions get, the better quality of life I can expect to have once I decide to fully enjoy retirement or to even semiretirement at an early age like 55.

Chapter 6
Index Funds

Why Would You Ever Follow A Money Manager When 80% Of These Lemmings Can't Beat The S&P 500 After Fees?
- Author

"Look Up At The Stars And Not Down At Your Feet."
- Stephen Hawking

Index funds are a great way to get broad market exposure of heavily traded securities with a low expense fee. It doesn't take any real strategy to own all the stocks in one market, sector, or industry, so the expenses should primarily come from trading, not on the prowess of the fund's manager. These funds, along with or instead of mutual funds, should make up a very solid base of assets that can help you attain instant diversity when you start investing for retirement. This beginning base should also help you maintain diversity as you grow into owning individual stocks and the single stock risk that comes with having exposure to any one stock that might go up 1000% over a decade or drop to 0.

SPDR funds, or "spider" funds, are exchange-traded funds (ETFs) that capture a particular segment of the market, one that you are specifically interested in, up to the whole market that might encompass a particular region. The S&P 500 index fund, the (SPY), is one of the best to own for beginning your retirement portfolio. It is made up of the 500 largest companies, measured by market cap, having common stock listed on the NYSE or the NASDAQ exchanges in the U.S. It is also one of the best benchmarks in the industry to use to measure your personal performance over the course of the years. If you feel uncomfortable in your ability to potentially outperform the top 500 U.S. companies over the course of any given year, I would not fault you for simply investing the majority of your investing assets in the SPY. This core holding, along with your personal preference for your exposure to bonds and international/emerging markets, are really the only three things in your retirement portfolio you would need besides your cash stash. You could certainly do worse than a simple strategy made up of a retirement portfolio based on 50% the SPY, 25% an emerging market ETF like the iShares Core MSCI Emerging Markets ETF (IEMG), and finally, a 25% stake in a bond fund like my Edward Jones recommended American Funds The Bond Fund of America (ABNDX) for example.

Here are a couple other popular broad-based ETF's that would make great starting funds among the 100's to 1000's of ETFs on the market at any one time. The Dow Jones Industrial Average (DIA) attempts to track the performance of the whole U.S. market. There is also the PowerShares QQQ ETF, the (QQQ), which is an index composed of the 100 largest international and domestic companies, excluding financial companies, listed on the Nasdaq stock exchange by market capitalization. The QQQ is seen as more of a play on how the technology sector is performing compared to the rest of the market.

Investors can also take advantage of broad market exposure to individual sectors of the market by owning a sector ETF. This is one way to bet on a particular area of the market, that an investor thinks will do well over the coming years or simply for diversity, instead of trying to pick out individual winners and losers among the particular stocks in that sector. Here are a few examples of the hundreds to thousands of different ETF's in the market at any given time that try to encompass exposure to one particular specifically defined part of the market. The Global Real

Estate ETF (RWO), the Biotech ETF (SBI), the China ETF (GXC), the Dividend ETF (SDY), the MidCap 400 ETF (MDY), and on and on are a few good examples for specific exposure an investor would be interested in. Many times a well-named ETF expresses exactly what the ETF's goals are, making it easier for investors to pick out several ETF's from their names only that appear to be what the investor is looking for. After you find a few good names of funds that sound exactly like what you are looking for, then go take a look at the funds top 10 holdings to finalize which fund you ultimately prefer the best. Individual brokers, like Charles Schwab for example, also tend to have a lot of ETF's of their own creation that they offer based on what their customers perceived needs are. Charles Schwab has a variety of company based ETF's with low fees, and no transaction costs, if bought with a Schwab account built for their customers.

While the lists of available funds can be a bit overwhelming at first, this should not ultimately dissuade an investor because, as you grow into investing, it ultimately makes investing more fun. Its great to be able to pick and choose specifically what you want to place bets on during any particular time period, and more than likely, you should be able to find an ETF or two that have good exposure to that particular asset class you are interested in. I find it fun at the start of each new year to try and imagine what that particular new year will bring, and how that will affect stocks specifically over that year. This can be a big deal especially if there were recent political elections or maybe oil had a huge run up or down the previous year. The ultimate goal is to try to increase my exposure to those areas that I think will do well over the coming year as I make my new investments, as long as I stay diversified, or to trim former winners or losers to re-invest in a diversified portfolio.

Lots of events can influence these decisions including recent political elections and what the new President might focus on including healthcare, infrastructure, tariffs, regulations, or any number of other issues. I also like to look at some of the losers of the last year, from the top companies in the S&P 500 that might be due for a rebound, just the same as for individual sector ETF's which might be due for a pullback after a tremendous year. I try to keep my trading and turnover low over the course of the year for most of my retirement portfolio with many of my core holdings bought to be held for decades at a time. However, I am proactive in trying to update my portfolio each and every year to try to keep it in alignment with my retirement goals along with satisfying my short-term trading desires.

There are also 11 main sector ETF's at this time that capture the main areas of the markets that are very useful if you want to add exposure to one particular sector without trying to pick out the biggest winners in that group. These ETF's are also very useful in rebalancing a portfolio at the end or at the beginning of a year. Let us say that energy had a marvelous year and utilities had a poor year in one particular year. At the end of the year, if you want to get your portfolio allocations better in line with your long term goals, you might sell a winning energy stock or ETF and simply invest those funds straight into a basic Utilities ETF without having to do any research on which utility stock you liked the best at that particular time. Sector ETFs are very useful for gaining exposure to areas of the market an investor really doesn't want to put a lot of time and effort into at that time, but wants exposure to it for diversification.

Here are the 11 main sector ETF's, although they will be changing soon, according to the GICS classification that are the easiest way to play the broader parts of the market after you have your initial base of whole market index funds or mutual funds set up and want to start getting more specific in your yearly investments. The Information Technology Sector (XLK), the Financials Sector (XLF), the Health Care Sector (XLV), the Communications Services Sector (XLC), the Energy Sector (XLE), the Materials Sector (XLB), the Industrials Sector (XLI), the Consumer Staples Sector (XLP), the Consumer Discretionary Sector (XLY), the Utilities Sector (XLU), and the Real Estate Sector (XLRE). As your portfolio grows and develops over time, try to have some numbers in mind for allocations and percentages for each sector, and use your IRA and 401k contributions to help bring the percentages close to being in line with your long-term desires.

Of course, different brokers or advisors could have their own versions of sector funds that they would recommend, but the basic idea is the same whatever sector funds you might want to use to invest in different parts of the market. Schwab could have a technology fund that would have a more desirable mix of technology stocks to you that you would prefer over the XLK for example. The expense ratios and performances will differ keep in mind, so be aware of that if you wanted to have an ETF with a higher weighting of Apple (AAPL) stock in it, or if you wanted a more balanced technology ETF where all of the technology stocks make up approximately 3% of the holdings with periodic rebalancing.

Also, ETF's and individual sectors can change over time as Real Estate was originally considered part of the Financial Sector, but it has now split off into its own recognized category now. Also, in September of 2018, the GICS Telecommunications Services Sector was renamed the Communications Sector and featured a shuffling around of approximately 200 stocks into new sectors like the former Telecommunications Services Sector, which used to be dominated by stocks like AT&T (T) and Verizon (VZ). The new Communications Sector will have stocks like The Walt Disney Company (DIS), Facebook Inc. (FB) and Alphabet Inc. (GOOGL) added to it, which will be a major change for many investors and institutions. These changes will result in the need for many investors to look at rebalancing their portfolios after figuring out how they want to weight different sectors of the market now after 200 stocks play musical chairs and move to different sectors. The world will continue to change and grow, so don't be afraid to grow and change your portfolio over time also to take advantage of new situations.

Chapter 7
Preparing For Single Stock Risk

Above All Else, Be Original.
- Author

"Innovation Distinguishes Between A Leader And A Follower."
- Steve Jobs

      Here is how I currently try to divvy up my allocations amongst the 11 different sectors, along with a bond division, while owning some index funds, half a dozen mutual funds, and about 30-40 individual stocks. The technical names according to the current GICS classification standard along with my current weightings goals are Information Technology 15%, Financials 15%, Health Care 15%, Communications Services 15%, Industrials 6%, Materials 6%, Consumer Discretionary 6%, Energy 6%, Consumer Staples 6%, Utilities 5%, Real Estate 3%, and finally a 2% position in bonds. These are the general weighting goals that I currently am aiming towards, although active trading and favoring sectors throughout the year leads me to make several key changes at the start of every new year when I load in my family's yearly IRA deposits.

At the end of 2018, with the new GICS sector classifications firmly in place, I plan on making final changes to my allocation goals and percentages to better represent the types of stocks I want to own in each sector now that sectors like the newly created Communications Sector will be a much more important part of the market than the old Telecommunications Sector used to be. Besides having exposure to all the different sectors of the market, I also seek to try to have my portfolio balanced around an 80% exposure to primarily to domestic assets with approximately 20% in international markets assets.

I generally try to maintain about 30-40 individual stocks in my portfolio, about 2-4 individual stocks per sector, while trying to ultimately stay diversified as my individual stocks should complement my core mutual and index funds. Generally, I like to look for a sector leader that I particularly like with a good solid long-term core bet. After my anchor, I try to look more for a potential value play, that I believe might be undervalued by the market, and that has a good shot at making a full comeback into favor with the market over the coming years. This gets you to about 20 individual stocks with another 10 spots for a second core leadership stock in several key sectors like technology or a sector or two that you have a particular knowledge about or love for. The particular sector that I personally love to look at and bet on with additional bets, especially as the year progresses, is the heath care sector, where I might have half a dozen different holdings as the year progresses. The final 5-10 stocks I save for speculative small cap stocks (think preclinical health care companies in my case) or beaten down giants (crash and burn companies) like Valeant Pharmaceuticals International which has since been renamed into Bausch Health Companies Inc. (BHC), or the General Electric Company (GE) that I try to make a bet or two on each year.

    A lot of these speculative stocks are 3-5 year projects, and most times I try to slowly build a position in them over a year or two with half a position buys of the company's stock several times over the course of a year or two. This helps me build a bigger position over time, and moderates my entry price, as a lot of times these stocks have not reached a bottom yet when I get fully interested in them. Also, preclinical programs can have many ups and downs for their stocks based on data presentations, partnerships, FDA signals, and especially their current cash position as they need to raise money periodically until they have commercial programs to rely on for future funding. Many preclinical programs typically take 3-5 years to approach commercialization, if they can get through Phase I, II, and III FDA clinical paths, so investors need to learn patience, along with the ability to hold through major price movements based on data or FDA interventions. Crash and burn projects like the General Electric Company (GE) can take a good year or two to find a bottom from where you initially might think a bottom is. Also, they may need at least a year or two of good solid recovery years before the market deigns to give them proper respect again also along with a better P/E ratio more in line with peers.

    I find that speculative stocks are a great way to find adrenaline in playing the market, besides bull and bear runs, but always try to keep the positions reasonable. This way, if they fizzle out, it doesn't bring your entire portfolio to its knees, or single handedly kill your performance against the S&P 500 for the year. I find it difficult to get my holdings a lot higher than 30-40 stocks because it quickly becomes hard to track all the different events affecting each individual sector, along with my winners and losers, in each category.

Throughout the year, I typically end up trying to sell positions that I don't fully believe in anymore, or take profits from stocks that I think might have run too far too fast, to re-enforce laggards in my portfolio that I think are still due for a bounce, or to initiate new positions in new stocks that become attractive to me over the year. Some of the most exciting new stocks I try to look at each year are the latest mergers and acquisition scenarios, which often times involve arbitrage situations that I love trying to take advantage of several times a year.

    At the end of every year, I try to take a thorough analysis of my holdings, using an Excel spreadsheet, to see what sectors have become bloated, and which have suffered over the course of year. I use my start of the year IRA contributions to help even things out towards my long-term allocation goals along with maybe selling one or two individual stocks, or merely taking profits, to re-invest in the sectors that I feel I am lacking in after the trading of the past year. Try to always keep your ultimate target allocations in perspective, and don't be alarmed if you find you want to change your sector percentages as your investments grow over time along with market and changes in society as you age. Just try to be aware of where you currently stand, and where you want to ultimately stand, by making at least yearly examinations with an advisor if you choose, or by making a detailed spreadsheet of your holdings, which you can use to easily see your sector, international, and bond exposures.

Chapter 8
The Information Technology Sector

The Greatest Wisdom Can Come From The Smallest Voice.
- Author

"Money Is Not The Only Answer, But It Makes A Difference."
- Barack Obama

      The Information Technology Sector is one of the most important sectors for young investors to start getting exposure to because it continues to shape and define our world. I would think a 15% allocation of your portfolio would be a good starting point at this time, although sector shakeups like the Telecommunications Services becoming the Communications Sector in September of 2018, along with approximately 200 stocks switching sectors, will have me fully re-evaluate my allocations and percentages again at the start of 2019. Also, know that a lot of names that you might think trade in the Technology Sector actually might trade in other sectors like the Consumer Discretionary Sector for Amazon.com Inc. (AMZN), or the Communications Sector for stocks such as Netflix Inc. (NFLX). This way, if you wanted to go heavier than my recommended 15% Technology Sector exposure, I would try to grab a couple more technology driven names in other sectors instead of traditional plays in those spaces.

    Over time, I think technology's growth and the way it continues to change the world across different industries, means that companies will continue to switch sectors, and whole new sectors will possibly even be created to deal with the newest innovations in technology stocks. Regardless of what sectors these types of stocks are in, young investors especially should find a way to get some exposure to a wide variety of them in their portfolios, even at high P/E multiples, because they will have the years and decades to hold the stocks while they hopefully grow into their valuations. The main ETF for this sector that I like to look at is the XLK, if you wanted to start a general base of investment in a variety of technology stocks, although there are a hundred others out there that might fit any given investor's wants and needs better for different reasons.

Regardless of how you think technology companies will grow and change over time, you need exposure to the sector even if you think technology is doomed to crash and burn like it did in the dot.com era when investors paid outrageous prices for internet stocks that had little to no earnings. There are many out there convinced (and with good cause) that valuations for many cutting edge technology companies are astronomical, and they would caution any investor against investing in these companies until valuations come more into line with actual earnings. High P/E ratios for many of the hottest companies out there is one good reason why I would suggest getting into some of these companies as early on in your retirement savings as possible, so that they have plenty of time to grow into their multiples over time, if they continue to dominate like the investor believes.

    The first individual stock that I most likely would recommend for anyone beginning to build their retirement portfolio, after their core base of mutual funds and index funds, would be the stock of Apple Inc. (AAPL). As the only FAANG stock still left in the all important Technology sector after this coming fall of 2018, it continues to be a great value compared to other high end technology stocks while it continues to innovate and dominate the landscape over time. Make things easy when you start your investing and go with a consensus pick, before you branch out later on, or decide to sell it in favor of a better opportunity later on. A few other great core stocks in this sector include Microsoft Corp. (MSFT) and Cisco Systems Inc. (CSCO), which would also make nice potential core positions in the space if you are not on the Apple bandwagon. Here's how these stocks compare to each other.

Technology	Market Cap	P/E	Forward P/E	PEG	Dividend Yield
Apple	$675B	11.71	11.44	0.90	2.05%
Microsoft	$748B	23.26	21.93	1.70	1.89%
Cisco	$185B	16.86	13.52	1.84	3.21%

Table by Trent Welsh

Besides a high-flying technology stock like Apple, I also like to try to find a value buy or two in the sector as a core holding, that I think is due for a catch-up trade. A stock that fit the bill for me recently has been International Business Machines (IBM). Here's a quick look at some of the reason's why I like this stock as a value play and long-term value investment for the Technology Sector of my portfolio.

IBM Value Case

IBM has been floundering now for years since its glory days before the dot.com era. Since then, it has struggled to remain relevant and has just had its first profitable quarter in years in early 2018. It has also been reeling from long-time investor Warren Buffett's exit from the stock in late 2017 and early 2018. Many of the large technology giants that have survived from 10 years ago have figured out how to successfully transition into the current environment including Microsoft (MSFT), Cisco Systems (CSCO), Apple (AAPL), and others with some being faster and some slower as the survivors seem eventually to figure out how to flourish once again. With a value stock like IBM, it is about impossible to time when a turnaround in the stock will officially occur, so a lot of times I put these project plays in my long term IRA account and try to buy in at several different times throughout the year to get a better shot at hitting near a bottom in the stock price. Once in my IRA account, I like to try and forget about stocks like IBM, as they play out their turnaround story, confident that they will eventually figure it out while enjoying the nice dividends along the way.

Performance	1 Year	3 Year	5 Year	10 Year
IBM	-6.33%	-16.9%	-26.4%	13.18%
Microsoft	43.54%	125.6%	194.3%	282.3%
Cisco	34.29%	50.14%	64.42%	96.47%
Apple	27.30%	46.86%	209.7%	675.8%
S&P 500	14.32%	32.07%	67.08%	124.1%

Table by Trent Welsh

Here's some reasons that I think IBM might be ready for a recovery and potential catch-up trade over the next 5-10 years as a long-term potential value play. According to the company's website, IBM inventors received a record 9,043 patents in 2017, which was IBM's 25th consecutive year of U.S. patent leadership. Not only that, over half of IBM's patents in 2017 were granted for leading technology advancements in areas like cybersecurity, blockchain, AI, cloud computing, and quantum computing. IBM is at the forefront, and in the mix, of many cutting edge technologies. If it ever figures out how to properly monetize any of these leadership positions properly, look out above as the stock will finally have a concrete reason for investors to hang their hats on when buying into the turnaround story.

Big data is a major opportunity for technology companies as gathering and effectively using data has really benefitted companies like Facebook (FB). Companies like Facebook seem so knowledgeable about their customer bases that they can effectively target them with ads that matter to the base that the competition can't match. This has allowed Facebook to grab vast swaths of advertising market share while maintaining premium pricing for advertising to its user base. IBM's big data innovation is called Watson, which is currently being used across many industries across the globe including Financial Services, Health Care, and the Internet of Things, just to name a few.

It's also a leader in facilitating the build-out of blockchain technology for the banking industry and numerous other services such as shipping and food storage. Instead of hopping on the Bitcoin and crypto currency trains, IBM is using its blockchain leadership position to help lead the way in how the technology will be changing every day life with real world applications. In banking for example, its helping set up crypto currencies for international banks to use in helping speed up cross-border transactions in seconds instead of days. By using a crypto currency as an intermediary, it is helping solve a lot of cross-border issues such as potentially no longer needing to store proper amounts of local and international currency at banks on a border. I am not sure if the Bitcoin (or the thousands of other crypto currencies) craze will continue to draw investors, or if they will ultimately crash and burn like companies in the dot.com era did, but I'm pretty certain that the underlying blockchain technology, developed by companies like IBM, behind these products will shape and define how business is done around the world not only for banks, but for food services, shipping, and eventually a million other possible applications. The question with IBM though still remains unfortunately. Can they find a way to monetize their advantage and bring the bacon home for investors? This uncertainty is why I believe IBM still trades at such a tremendous discount to the market.

    With stocks like IBM, you never know when they will get their mojo back, whether it will be later in 2018 or in 2025. However, a stock like this I am confortable putting into my IRA account and forgetting about until retirement, as I don't have any current plans on trading it over the next couple of decades unless the story really changes and goes downhill. I like the long-term potential of the stock at this time, along with the nice 3.5%-4% dividend it pays, while it might have a very attractive upswing coming if it can increase its profits and find a way to shift investor sentiment its way again.

Finally, there should be room in your portfolio for a speculative stock or two in the technology sector that is small now, or super risky now, that might contain explosive growth for the future. As a major part of many investor's portfolios, technology is a place where a lot of people should take a shot at a down the road future tech company that appeals to them and what they think the future holds. Also, as I finish off fully diversifying other sectors of my portfolio, I am very tempted to load up on small positions of an additional half a dozen stocks in this category. I am only considering this move though now that I have got most of the rest of my portfolio where I want it, and would like to take some more small shots on companies that I think might be game changers moving forward, especially in the technology and health care sector for me in particular.

Alibaba Group Holding Limited (BABA) I put into the speculative category primarily because it is a Chinese company with its IPO happening only a couple of years ago. It is listed on a U.S exchange though, and has a lot more transparency than most Chinese companies, which makes it a lot safer bet than the majority of Chinese companies in my opinion. I plan on moving this company up to a more core position, and out of the speculative realm soon as its earnings and performance have solidified, and the company now is one of the most predictable and reliable among tradable Chinese stocks. For my International exposure, it is one of my key holdings as I feel the desire to find a way to get exposure to the high-octane Chinese market besides a broad based ETF. Here are a few other speculative technology stocks that I have looked at and traded including Spotify (SPOT), Snap Inc. (SNAP), VMware Inc. (VMW), and Pivotal Software (PVTL). With advances in this area coming fast and furious, there are literally almost hundreds of stocks that an investor could make an argument for, which I think is a great thing.

Speculative	Market Cap	P/E	Forware P/E	PEG	Dividend Yield
Alibaba	$339B	38.98	25.13	1.54	NA
Spotify	$19B	NA	NA	NA	NA
Snap	$7B	NA	NA	NA	NA
VMware	$54B	21.96	20.97	2.01	NA
Pivotal	$4B	NA	NA	NA	NA

Table by Trent Welsh

I try to maintain most of my speculative bets around 1% more or less of my total portfolio value (Alibaba is an exception) so that massive declines might make for a bad day, but they won't result in losing any sleep over my performance over the course of a year. If a speculative bet misses, it is easy enough to move on with the loss. However, if a speculative stock hits, I have a great option to sell half or my whole position and move on to the next bet, or to let the position ride into a longer term bet on the company that becomes a bigger and bigger position in my portfolio. The risk though doesn't become much more than the original 1% exposure of my original investment even if it explodes in tremendous gains.

Thus, if a stock quintuples over the year from $2 to $10 and goes from ~1% of my portfolio to ~5% of my portfolio, I am fine with selling out of the position altogether and moving on if I like other opportunities better after the tremendous return. I am also fine with riding that 5% position knowing that if it crashes to $0, even though I lose 5% of my portfolio from the highs, I ultimately lose only my 1% bet in money that I actually invested. These types of stocks can be the stocks that allow you to retire at 55 instead of 65 like Amazon (AMZN) when it first became a publically traded company. I think many investors in the market are either much too conservative, or much too risky in how they trade and invest for their retirement. I'm much more of a fan of having a solid core base of investments to build around while taking yearly shots along the way at greatness.

Chapter 9
The Financial Sector

Listen To Longs, Listen To Shorts, Then Be Strong Enough To Forge Your Own Path.
- Author

"I Will Tell You How To Become Rich. Close The Doors. Be Fearful When Others Are Greedy. Be Greedy When Others Are Fearful."
- Warren Buffet

    A very important sector of the market, which many investors might want to have a larger than normal exposure to, is the all-important Financial Sector. This sector includes stocks in banks, trading companies for securities, some major holding companies, bank services, and insurance companies to name a few interesting sections of this group. Its main sector ETF is the (XLF), which I like to trade around if I need to make general adjustments in my retirement accounts, as I try to set my target goal to around 15% of my total portfolio. In September of 2016, the XLF spun off the real estate portion of the fund, which was approximately 20% of the XLF at the time. This move was consistent with GICS reclassification of real estate's newly elevated status as its own independent sector of the market. Changes like this are very important to monitor because they can immediately alter how you want to allocate funds across your portfolio over the rest of the year. During these reconfiguration years, I find there is a greater need to rebalance my portfolio at the end of the year, and the beginning of the next year when I put my yearly IRA funds to work, so that I continue to have holdings set in accord with my new allocation goals as another sector needs to be worked in.

Financials make up the core backbone of many markets, both domestically and internationally, by helping to facilitate trading across the globe whether it is in cash, materials, or stocks. Whether the global market is moving up or down at any one time, investors will continue to move money and change strategies based on their risk preferences as one generation gives over to the next generation.

This sector has many meaningful influences on it, although rate sensitivity is the main concern for a significant portion of the sector in normal non-crisis times. In general, as the Fed hikes or lowers rates over any particular year, so the rates over longer periods of time also generally change as well as the 2-year, the 10-year, and the 30 year rates also tend to change in the same direction. These changes can directly correlate with how banks can potentially make more or less money by lending funds out to customers based on the new rate spreads. The way that rates tend to increase over time gives investors what is known as the yield curve. The interest rate a bank might make on a 2-year loan might be 2.5%, a 10-year loan 3%, and a 30-year loan might be 4.5%, which gives you a yield curve when the points are plotted on a graph. Many factors go into these curves though and there are plenty of much more interesting instances in the market such as flat yield curves or inverted yield curves, which can be used to help predict recessions or other upcoming economic changes.

    This sector tends to get big pullbacks once or twice a decade though from scandals, global recessions, or even individual political and financial crises in particular countries like most recently Italy and Greece. Managing big money is an incredible incentive for greed and manipulation not only for bankers, but for governments as well. It also is a prime place to make "leveraged" bets, or margin bets, where the debt involved in a deal is greater than the equity involved in the deal. This includes borrowing money, while paying interest of course, to make additional bets on the stock of a company for example. An investor can also borrow money to short the stock of a particular company as well. This bet comes with unlimited potential losses as stocks can always go higher, and can never reach an ending $0 point like playing the long stock game can.

There are also securities in the market where an investor can place money on a security that moves 2 times or 3 times the volatility of the instrument that it is linked to like the VIX (CBOE Volatility Index) for example. Making different types of leveraged bets can result in huge returns over a short period of time, but of course can also lead to complete losses, or worse, if things go completely against what the investor is expecting. These types of bets have been a big reason for some of the great losses in the sector in the past, and for some of the giant moves in index funds over short periods of time as unexpected events can multiply the selling quickly which has resulted in the past in sudden market corrections and near crashes.

Another issue to be aware of is that a lot of trading on the markets now is done automatically by computers with buy and sell levels set into the computer using algorithms and triggers. This can help traders take advantages of potential arbitrage situations, make buy or sell calls according to market momentum, or trade immediately off of the latest news releases. The problem with taking the human element out of trading like this is that major unexpected market moves can result in massive volume in stocks as computers are triggered across the globe at the same time. Suddenly hundreds of computers get triggered to start selling everything at the exactly same time, hugely exacerbating an issue where humans might have been slower to sell, or might even have stepped in to buy the rapid unexplained drop in the market.

For example, if there is a flash crash where the Dow Jones (DJIA) crashes over 1,000 points in less than an hour, this might be a trigger point for emotionless computers around the world to automatically hit the SELL button, even if there is no definable reason or news apparent for the flash crash. Instead of thousands of traders each examining the issue and making a conscious decision to sell everything, you might have thousands of computers hitting the sell button automatically because some number was hit to trigger an event over some short-term time period. Traders might take a look at the market and say, there is no real reason for this selloff, so it might possibly be a great buying opportunity, but computers might not even give it a thought and would just automatically sell. So, instead of the Dow Jones (DJIA) crashing 1,000 points and some traders stepping in to buy their favorite stocks hand over fist and halting the selloff, computers continue to sell as further triggers are hit, and maybe even further exacerbate the issue with sells bringing down the market 1,500 points instead of traders creating a rebound.

These flash crashes continue to occur in different forms, more often than you would think, and can be a great reason to have some extra cash on hand, especially when there is no big news that comes along with the crashes. However, timing a market bottom is virtually impossible to do as it is very hard to say if tomorrow will lead to another 1,000 or 1,500 point loss again in the markets, or if the market will rebound 1,000 points instead. When you can't point to any significant event for the crash in the first place, it is pretty much a tossup as to what will happen the following day as there is no actual bad news to be fixed or explained. This is why I almost always try to maintain a low cash balance in my retirement accounts. I am a much bigger fan of the time value of money argument, which argues that the more time I have my money in stocks in the stock market, the more money I will ultimately end with over an extended period of time. I've tried timing the market before in unusual situations and usually fare worse off than if I had just stuck to my guns.

If there is a 20%-30% market correction, especially over a short time period, this is the time when I consider bringing regular spending money into the markets. The best times to bet on a rebound, a lot of times I find, are when the market overreacts to global issues like a Greece or Italy political crisis, or on what might happen months or years from now like when investors start to fear OPEC and its allies might increase oil production when its annual summer meeting comes around.

Instead of using my extra cash that month for a bigger student loan payment, or having a nice chunk of extra cash in my checking account, I might take the opportunity to reallocate that money into the markets after a serious pullback. I'm not talking about betting any great amount of money, or the kids tuition money for example, means maybe the economy might be entering into a recession or maybe there is a sustained downturn coming to the market. These small extra bets every few months if the downturn continues might help you receive an outsized gain in the following months if the market rebounds as I might predict. And if the market doesn't turn around and instead stays lower for longer or turns into a full blown recession, you only have a small amount of extra money in the market that won't change much for you in the long run anyway.

    I do these extra bets through a taxable account so that when the market has sufficiently recovered enough that I want my money back, I sell my index fund or ETF for example, and put the money and profits back towards my student loans or back into my checking account. I then take note of the additional taxes that I will be liable for in the coming year on the capital gains the market just gave me when I sold for a profit. You can also balance out the capital gain by selling a losing stock in the taxable account to offset the gain for tax purposes also. Just be aware of the tax implications and plan for them accordingly and you should be fine. Also, don't use your credit cards to make these bets, or use money you can't afford to lose, because sometimes the downturn in the market might go on for years at a time for no great reason, and it will be very hard to sell out of your current position without incurring the losses from buying into a market correction too early. The market continues to make new historical highs given enough time, so it is just a matter of time until you should get your money back with profits according to the past almost 100 years. However, make sensible small bets that you can afford to wait on over an extended time period, if your timing is horrible, or if the market decides to enter into a 10-year bear market.

OK, back to the topic at hand, after getting your initial exposure to some of the financial sector through your starting mutual funds or general index funds, you might want to take a more specific shot on some of the companies in the sector that you feel might be better bets for long-term performance than the general Financial Sector ETF (XLF). With approximately 15% of your portfolio located in this sector, it should give investors plenty of space for 2-3 individual stock plays, to start with, besides your core holdings.

As for your core holding, it is best just to stick with one of the big banks or trading companies that should continue to grow and thrive in good times and easily survive through harder times like a financial crisis, rate manipulations, or another mortgage crisis. Here are some of my favorites to hold and trade over the past few years including Bank of America (BAC), Citigroup Inc. (C), JPMorgan Chase & Co. (JPM),

Goldman Sachs Group Inc. (GS), and The Charles Schwab Corporation (SCHW).

Financials	Market Cap	P/E	Forward P/E	PEG	Dividend Yield
Bank of America	$241B	10.68	9.6	0.90	2.44%
Citigroup	$128B	8.11	7.91	0.60	3.42%
JPM	$323B	11.27	10.47	1.32	3.30%
Goldman Sachs	$63B	6.78	6.7	0.28	1.89%
Charles Schwab	$55B	18.24	16.72	0.67	1.28%

Table by Trent Welsh

With trading volatility on the rise finally, after a couple of slower trading years, I have focused lately more on building a large core position in Goldman Sachs (GS), which has a nice P/E and should benefit more from increased active trading like Charles Schwab (SCHW) will, than a typical bank stock should. With interest rates likely on the rise over 2018 and for the foreseeable future, regular bank stocks have done well and should continue to do potentially remarkably well also since the lows around the middle of 2016.

Once I have a core holding or two that I like a lot, I like to keep my eyes open for more of a value play in the sector. One of my favorite value plays for the past few years has been HSBC Holdings PLC (HSBC). This is because of the tremendous dividend yield it sports, along with the fact that I use it as one of my main holdings for some of my international stocks, featuring exposure to the United Kingdom as well as Hong Kong. I consider an international pick like this as a kind of bonus pick in a sector a lot of times in addition to a regular core holding or two and value play or two as it helps me boost my international exposure. Many times I'll have an international stock in my IRA long-term account, while I actively trade in and out of the domestic big bank names in the sector in my 401k account, depending on which I think will do better over the next few years, as each have their own strengths and weaknesses.

HSBC qualifies for me as a value stock because of the different scandals and rate fixing issues that the company continues to work its way through along with continued Brexit concerns. Brexit is the event where Britain is moving away from the Euro in favor of its own currency again along with a general move away from the Eurozone alliances and treaties. All of these issues have weighed heavily on the stock in the past, and have given it a very attractive P/E multiple as it continues to earn decent cash flow even though the cash flow has been under pressure. HSBC is committed to keeping its dividend payments at their current very attractive levels though and has little viability risk, which makes it a nice value in my mind instead of a riskier speculation play. While fines, legal matters, and Brexit continue to dog the stock, I see nothing that will ultimately bring the company to its knees. A couple hundred million or billion in fines a year is not too big of a deal in my mind for a company trading at such depressed multiples, with the cash flow and assets that the company has, especially when most big banks are all facing many of the same issues across the globe. As rates continue to rise and earnings continue to grow again for the bigger banks, I like to try to trade in and out of the other bank stocks as I hold firm to my HSBC value stock and current GS core holding.

    Finally, for a more speculative play in the space I continue to look at some bigger international financial institutions that have been under pressure over the past few years with a possible turnaround in place in the years to come. In the past, this play was HSBC, but after its nice turnaround over the past year or two, I consider it a more stable international play instead of a more risky speculative play. Currently on my list of more international speculative plays in the space I am looking at is the German big bank Deutsche Bank AG (DB) along with Credit Suisse Group AG (CS), which have yet to recover from the continued underperformance they have experienced in the space. Here is a look at how the stocks have performed over the past few years compared to HSBC.

International Value Plays	P/E	Dividend Yield	1-Year Stock Performance	3-Year Stock Performance	5-Year Stock Performance
Deutsche Bank	NA	1.58%	-36%	-58%	-68%
Credit Suisse	20.8	1.89%	0.8%	-47%	-46%
HSBC	15.7	5.91%	-1.5%	4.6%	-15%

Table by Trent Welsh

A lot of the same issues that have plagued banks like HSBC (HSBC) over the past are also affecting Deutsche Bank (DB) and Credit Suisse (CS), but soon might be passing. It is always hard to predict bottoms, so I have started building a position in Deutsche Bank with small purchases over the course of the middle and back half of 2018 as I am in no hurry to get overexposed to a stock that might have more downside left in it.

Some other forms of speculative plays in the financial sector that might interest investors could be some of the more local smaller community banks. These are becoming more attractive as the government continues to work on rolling back and modifying the Dodd-Frank Wall Street Reform and Consumer Protection Act issues, which have inadvertently severely limited the prospects of these banks over the past few years as they have a lot of the same capital requirements and stringent stress testing that the big banks have. This over-regulation in the sector over the past 5-10 years has gone a long way towards killing off many of the smaller community banks that can't compete effectively with the large banks any more when subjected to the same stringent regulatory rules.

However, some new reforms over the past year or so, with more changes possibly coming, have done a lot to disrupt excess regulations on these smaller financial institutions. Congress has been working on removing and reforming parts of Dodd-Frank with an eye towards giving local community banks a fair chance to compete and flourish again against the global multinational banks. Here are some of the more interesting community banks that I have considered investing in recently with some small purchases coming in the middle to back half of 2018 planned. I have held off so far because Dodd-Frank issues are still evolving and I like my current big bank holdings in the space a lot. But I feel some changes coming soon to my portfolio as the environment continues to look better and better for many of these community banks. Here are a few of the community banks that I am most interested in at this time including Comerica Inc. (CMA), First Financial Bankshares Inc. (FFIN), and Guaranty Bancorp (GBNK).

Community Banks	Market Cap	P/E	Forward P/E	PEG	Dividend Yield
Comerica	$11B	10.63	9.65	0.53	3.46%
First Financial	$4B	27.66	25.79	NA	1.46%
Guaranty Bancorp	$873M	18.92	15.57	1.89	2.18%

Table by Trent Welsh

As with your other individual stock holdings in different sectors, try to have your core investments in the bigger name stocks along with a value play or two and keep the speculative stock holdings on the lower end until actual regulations and changes come around instead of just the guessing game of if and when they will.

Chapter 10
The Health Care Sector

Shorting The Market As A Long-Term Strategy Is Like Playing Dinosaurs, It Works Until You Get Blasted By An Asteroid.
- Author

"Identify Your Problems But Give Your Power And Energy To Solutions."
- Tony Robbins

    The Health Care sector is the last of my big portfolio sector positions, which I try to maintain around 15% of my total portfolio with limited success. At the end of almost every year I have to try to pare down my holdings in this sector, to redistribute to other areas, as I love researching and investing in this area more than most other sectors. I tend to gravitate towards making more bets in this area, along with bigger bets, as I tend to know the stocks better and follow many companies in this space. My usual investment routine for many of the other sectors is to follow a few basic core stocks that particularly intrigue me, and then to look at a few other companies in the space throughout the year if big news starts hitting the space due to M&A or new highs or lows in the sector etcetera.

The main sector ETF for Health Care is the (XLV), which I almost never use, as I am continually trying to trade in and out of smaller drug candidate companies as the year progresses besides having a couple main core stocks to anchor the my holdings. This sector is a great sector for many investors to have most of their exposure in the ETF (XLV) as most investors don't want to put the time and effort into all the drama and intrigue of individual companies trying to develop drugs in the Health Care field. These developments can be very complex when you add in additional variables such as the FDA, along with political concerns over pricing and controls, which at any time can put pressure on all the players in the space regardless of their prospects. For most investors, having most of their funds in the ETF will do with one potential core stock holding of a big name company along with a potential value play. Most investors should stay away from the more speculative side of this sector unless you are willing to put the time and effort into finding some of the hidden gems, and are prepared to follow the intricacies of dealing with the FDA and other issues that come up over the course of a year.

One of the benefits, or hindrances, of this sector is that a lot of the core companies are domestic names that are more immune from many international or global supply and demand issues along with foreign government turmoil concerns than other sectors. They shouldn't be too concerned with tariffs, or the rising or falling of rates in the market, or the general ups and downs of the market or oil as a whole. A financial crisis bringing down a good part of the market shouldn't have as much of an affect on whether or not a company can continue to sell insulin to patients over the course of a month or year. People need medicines regardless of how the market is performing, so this sector can act as a hedge against foreign market volatility as it is more concerned with sales of its products than how the dollar is doing versus the yen.

One political concern over recent years though is the focus on price gouging and fraud by companies such as the former Valeant Pharmaceuticals, which has since renamed into Bausch Health Companies Inc. (BHC), and some of their unscrupulous employees. This has helped draw political attention to the sector, especially in election years, along with calls for price controls, closer scrutiny of rising drug prices, and the costs of health care in general. It seems that the sector has become a political stepping-stone during many election seasons with statements routinely causing 1%-3% drops in the sector just by mentions by prominent political figures on pricing concerns. This doesn't mean you can't continue to have a large exposure to the sector, it just means you have to be aware of what is going on and why a company making great profits in the sales of its drugs or the running of its hospitals can be under pressure through no fault of its own.

Once you have figured out your level of ETF or mutual fund involvement in this area, a quick look at the bigger names should lead you to decide if you want to aim more for a bigger player bent on growth and new products, or if you are looking for a more stable and dividend orientated giant that has numerous products on the market along with an extensive pipeline of potential drug candidates which could continue to produce results for years to come. Besides drug companies, you can get your healthcare exposure from a medical devices company, a company that runs hospitals, or some form of hybrid company that is more of a conglomerate.

Here's a sampling of some of the bigger names in the space that I have been interested in as some of my core holdings. Domestic names include Eli Lily and

Company (LLY), Medtronic plc (MDT), Johnson and Johnson (JNJ), UnitedHealth Group Inc. (UNH), and the international drug company Sanofi (SNY) for example.

Health Care	Market Cap	P/E	Forward P/E	PEG	Dividend Yield
Eli Lily	$118B	48.95	19.93	3.51	2.32%
Medtronic	$115B	24.75	16.65	2.92	2.34%
Johnson & Johnson	$337B	23.60	15.40	2.91	2.86%
UnitedHealth	$228B	20.54	18.49	1.30	1.52%
Sanofi	$106B	23.3	13.29	3.76	4.22%

Table by Trent Welsh

After you pick a main core holding or two besides your core ETF, you might consider a value play in the space that trades below its peers for one reason or another. One of my favorites in the past that fits this category for me has been Gilead Sciences Inc. (GILD), especially as the company has come down to earth after its miraculous hepatitas C drug Harvoni.

Gilead Value Case

In October of 2014, the U.S. Food and Drug Administration approved Harvoni for the treatment of hepatitis C infection in adults. This drug was miraculous in the fact that it wasn't just a treatment, or a functional cure, that worked like a cure as long as you continued to take the drug for the rest of your life. It was a cure that meant that once you successfully finished the treatment cycle, you were cured of hepatitis C for forever, and no longer needed to take Harvoni any more.

This cure was worth $10's of billions of dollars a year for Gilead as they could charge monopoly prices for the drug. They could charge huge prices because almost everyone who had hepatitis C naturally wanted to be free of it, and insurance companies had to make up the difference between what they charged their customers and the price of the drug treatment. This meant that for several years Gilead has made money hand over fist on their cure while competition was little to non-existent, and there was still a large population of people infected with hepatitis C across developed companies. Here's a look at how Gilead's stock has traded around its blockbuster hepatitis C drug's approval in late 2014.

Gilead's Harvoni	Quarterly Revenue	Approximate Stock Price
Mid 2013	$2.4B	$60
Mid 2014	$5B	$70
Mid 2015	$8.2B	$120
Mid 2016	$7.8B	$85
Mid 2017	$6.5B	$70
Mid 2018	$5.1B	$70

Table by Trent Welsh

Notice how the stock price rocketed up with peak sales of its Harvoni drug, in the first half-a-year up to the first full year of use, as everyone rushed to get cured, massively boosting the company's quarterly revenues at that time? After the initial rush finished off, sales started to markedly slow as less people needed to be cured, competition has since entered the space, and prices have come down due to effects like increased competition.

The market loves to overreact to many news items and events and you can see how predictable the stock price action was if you simply followed through with the expectation for what should happen with a blockbuster cure for a drug like Harvoni. These drugs are very rare and very lucrative so the overreaction to the upside should be predictably pretty great. The overreaction potentially to the downside might also be almost as impressive, now that revenues have come back down to pre-Harvoni levels along with the stock price. The difference between mid 2018 and mid 2014 is that Gilead does not have a huge potential drug in its pipeline and the hype associated with it, but instead, has the billions of dollars in revenues in its vault along with its most recent acquisition of Kite Pharma Inc. for just under $12 billion dollars in late 2017. It is yet to be seen if the former Kite Pharma's pipeline of candidates can ramp up investor enthusiasm for Gilead moving forward, along with Gilead's strong pipeline, or if the company will continue to trade sideways for another year or two as investors continue to find other places to put their hard-earned investing dollars.

While nothing can easily replace the miracle that was Harvoni, I think Gilead is in a great place at this time, as investor sentiment might have bottomed out with a hopeful overreaction to the downside already built into the stock. Gilead Sciences now trades with an incredible P/E value of 10.32 along with a forward P/E value of 11.42, which is an incredible value means it still has a lot of gunpowder in the company's pipeline for future drug innovation and success, especially after its Kite Pharma acquisition. Gilead Sciences is a great example to me of a market value opportunity right now that has long-term great potential upside from these depressed prices.

The speculative space in health care has a special place in my heart, as it is one of my favorite places to make long shot bets throughout the year. Small drug companies, with months to years left until they have a potential drug candidate to commercialize and make money on, can be some nice long term bets if you believe in the science and the market opportunity and are aware of the risk associated with these opportunities. Other ways to bet on this space are upcoming FDA decisions, clinical trial results, health care conference presentations, major partnerships with bigger companies, or maybe a turnaround story for stocks that have been beaten down 90% + from their highs for whatever reasons.

Here have been some of my favorite speculative bets over the past couple of years, which have made and lost me considerable money in short time periods, while I continue to improve and adapt my strategies. These companies include MannKind Corporation (MNKD), BioTelemetry Inc. (BEAT), Bausch Health Companies Inc. (BHC), Sarepta Therapeutics (SRPT), and Arrowhead Pharmaceutials (ARWR).

Speculative	Market Cap	P/E	Forward P/E	PEG	Dividend Yield
MannKind	$212M	NA	NA	NA	NA
BioTelemetry	$1.8B	82	30.52	NA	NA
Bausch	$7.2B	NA	5.41	NA	NA
Sarepta	$7.1B	NA	NA	NA	NA
Arrowhead	$1.1B	NA	11.41	NA	NA

Table by Trent Welsh

For these plays I typically look for something unique about the company, that sets it apart from the rest of the competition, that gives it a potential competitive advantage, at least for the short-term. For example, here are some of the main reasons I bought into some of the previous speculative companies in the past:

1. *A monopoly like presence in a space* is always something that immediately grabs my attention, as it did with the FDA approval of MannKind's inhalable insulin Afrezza. This became the only inhalable mealtime insulin on the market, with no competition coming in the immediate future. It had some built in competitive advantages like being convenient for a diabetic, by not needing to take a shot to deliver the

needed insulin, along with having a major health care company as a partner for Afrezza's commercial launch in Sanofi (SNY).

However, that's about where the positive aspects of this company ended as Sanofi's CEO who approved the MannKind partnership exited his job and was replaced by a new CEO who had had a negative experience with Pfizer Inc.'s (PFE) failed inhalable insulin drug Exubera in 2006. After about a year of slow and poor sales, Sanofi dropped Afrezza like a bad habit. This left MannKind with one approved product on the market along with the responsibility for promoting, commercializing, marketing, and selling Afrezza on its own. This also means that MannKind will be able to solely benefit from all the profits associated with the drug, means they won't have to share with a partner anymore, if they can ever get the drug profitable.

Afrezza comes with an infamous "black label" warning, based primarily on lung concerns just like what helped kill the drug Exubera when it was on the market, even though MannKind's drug overcomes many of the lung concerns that dogged Exubera. To say that sales of Afrezza have been anemic and disappointing in its first couple years of commercialization would be an understatement to just about anyone following the drug and its preclinical potential. A major healthcare company couldn't sell it, and even a positive update to the labeling by the FDA a couple years later didn't skyrocket sales either along with a brief TV advertising campaign. Afrezza has come a long way from where it began, both with Sanofi and MannKind on its own, but it still has a long ways to go before it will be anywhere near where I thought it could be when I really got interested in it before its FDA approval.

    Unfortunately for me, I have never sold a share of MannKind's stock as my original thesis is still intact as it continues to be a monopolistic drug with competitive advantages for a large diabetic market. This dedication to the stock and my thesis has lead to my biggest single stock loss over my investing career so far. The drug still is the only inhalable insulin on the market, it is still extremely easy to use, it has advantages over regular mealtime insulin built into its FDA label, and I believe there is still a niche in the enormous insulin market for a drug like this to succeed. However, this might not stop the company from going bankrupt in the meantime, or taking an additional 10 years for the drug to become profitable.

One other stock with a monopoly position in the health care space that I love is Sarepta Therapeutics (SRPT) in the Duchenne Muscular Dystrophy (DMD) space. It had a bear of a time getting FDA approval for its Exondys 51 drug, which has been described as an "exotic placebo" by some criticizing its clinical trial data results. With FDA approval of the drug looking dubious at best, parents of DMD kids organized and petitioned the FDA for approval of the drug. The Parent Project Muscular Dystrophy (PPMD) not only was successful in helping push the FDA into approving Sarepta's Exondys 51 drug, they were also successful in helping the FDA change its official guidelines for action on issues such as DMD, allowing for more accelerated approvals with rolling clinical trials that can be done over time, while potential life changing drugs get approved and on the market before all the regular required data is in and passed by the FDA. The Parent Project movement has helped Sarepta by setting the stage for an accelerated approval of its next DMD drug golodirsen, which treats another subset of the DMD market, as the FDA will find it very hard to say no to golodirsen after the success of Exondys 51 in the market.

Sarepta is gaining a huge competitive advantage in the space by getting its foot in the door, with outstanding sales over the past year exceeding most analyst expectations, with more drugs hopefully entering the market over the next few years for other portions of the DMD population. Sarepta is capitalizing on its opportunity, while most of its competition in the space is still 2-3 years away from possible commercial entrance into the space, or already has a partnership with Sarepta in place to share commercialization of possible future drugs.

I have had great success doubling down on 20%-30% pullbacks in the stock and taking profits after the stock hits new 52-week highs as it continues to increase its sales dramatically with DMD kid's parents waiting in the wings to oppose the FDA, or anyone else standing in the way of additional drug approvals. As I have now been able to successfully take nice profits in the stock a couple of times while still maintaining an overweight position in my portfolio, I am more inclined to let my profits ride as I go for outsized gains over the next couple years before the competition potentially becomes more of a threat.

However, I am always aware that all it takes is for one death to occur, that is directly attributed to Exondys 51, that would result in a halt to sales of the drug immediately along with cutting the stock price by

25-50% in a heart beat. That is why I began investing in this stock as a small position in my portfolio and used 20%-30% pullbacks to eventually build an oversized position in the stock over time. Building up my position on pullbacks and selling off some of my position when the stock reached new 52-week highs means that if a disaster does happen, I won't ultimately be losing all of my principle and gains, but mostly my profits as I have already cashed out most of my original principle amounts. At this point, it is much easier to rest easily at night and go for a jackpot win in letting my oversized position continue to ride longer than I usually would as I am a firm believer in the story over the next 2-3 years at least. These are the types of stocks that can help you crush the S&P 500 over a year and the types of stocks I try to bet on at least once or twice a year, especially on unjustified pullbacks in the stocks price in my mind at least.

2. *Possible groundbreaking science* that has years to go and huge risk, but also has that considerable upside if the company is successful in progressing a drug closer and closer to commercialization on terrific efficacy data and safety. One of my favorite stocks that could have groundbreaking science is Arrowhead Pharmaceuticals (ARWR), which is in the notoriously

difficult RNAi space, a space that many other companies have failed in over the years. Its interests have included drugs designed as "functional cures" for issues like Hepatitis B. Think about how successful Gilead has been with its Hepatitis C cure and the magnitude of profits it brought for that stock. A functional cure for Hepatitis B could be a gold mine for Arrowhead, which continues to diversify its treatment platform to many other possible treatments as well including lung issues and rare diseases.

Under its original ARO platform, the company's stock rose to around $25 a share in 2014 before pulling back to more moderate levels of $7-$8 a share in 2015 and 2016 as the science is so hard to count on. Then disaster hit in the back half of 2016, when a chimpanzee died over toxicity concerns in a preclinical study, causing the FDA to put a hold on Arrowhead's clinical trials over safety concerns. This toxicity issue, along with the FDA concerns, looked like too much for the company to easily overcome at that time. So Arrowhead literally abandoned its full pipeline of drug candidates based on the ARO RNAi platform, resulting in the stock dropping to a little over $1 a share by late 2016. By abandoning its old platform, it started completely over again from scratch using its new TRiM platform this time. The company had to start again in animal models but could at least work with HBV and other issues it had worked on for years under its ARO platform. As the science continues to progress and candidates close in on clinical trials in actual humans again, the stock has again rebounded up to the $7-$10 a share range as the data and safety are even better than the ARO platform at least at this time. Once again it is sitting in a comfortable range waiting to see if the science progresses or ultimately fails as a classic homerun stock.

Arrowhead Pharmaceuticals trades a lot of times around a $500 million to $1 billion market cap company, but if its science hits and its drug candidates make it to market, the market cap could easily reach into the $10's of billions. It could almost print money with a catalog of functional cures from the breadth and depth of its pipeline of candidates, which now looks to expand out past the liver and into areas such as the lung. Stocks like these can be fun to invest in and follow over the years, but try to keep your positions at a respectable level as they can encounter a FDA hold at anytime on a safety concern. Also, don't be afraid to take profits after nice bull runs along the way, and to reload up on noticeable pullbacks as many things can happen over the course of preclinical trials to commercialization, along with actual sales of approved drugs once they do hit the market.

3. *Partnership with a major company.* This is a pretty common situation for a lot of smaller health care companies trying to get a drug or device to market through the FDA approval process, which can take years, while not actually having any products to sell commercially. The company needs to periodically raise money while they develop their pipeline of candidates and partnerships are often efficient ways to do this while still maintaining the rights to many of their drug candidates.

In my previous cases, MannKind (MNKD) partnered with Sanofi (SNY) after the FDA's approval for the commercialization of its inhalable insulin Afrezza. This partnership lasted all of about a year before Sanofi dropped the drug and its commercialization rights, due to poor sales, leaving MannKind to fend for itself in future marketing and commercialization.

Arrowhead Pharmaceuticals (ARWR) has partnered with Amgen (AMGN) on a couple of its preclinical candidates that have yet to enter into human trials, although that is predicted to happen by the end of

2018, or by the beginning of 2019. Mere general mentions by Amgen of the possibility of progressing one of Arrowhead's partnered candidates in corporate slides have caused 20%+ moves in Arrowhead's stock when investors took note and bet on a potential milestone payment coming, or merely the validation that the preclinical candidate has the potential to progress towards commercialization. A lot of times these deals include the big pharmaceutical company taking over much of the R&D spending, development, and commercialization of a drug in exchange for paying the original company milestone payments and royalties on sales in certain markets if the drug eventually hits the market. Milestone payments can be very eventful days for the smaller drug companies stock as a lot of times they are cash strapped, and every step closer to commercialization is another step towards a cash flow stream for their bottom line that they don't have to support with their own commercialization efforts.

    Another example of an opportunistic partnership is with cardiac monitoring company BioTelemetry (BEAT). Apple Inc. (AAPL) partnered up with Stanford University for a Heart Study featuring the Apple's watch, along with its own custom built App, and BioTelemetry's cardiac monitoring devices and software. Apple's use of BioTelemetry's equipment and software helps validate its position as an industry leader and helps open the company up for further expanding into clinical trial opportunities that involve heart monitoring, or eventually other health concerns such as diabetes . A potential long shot bonus with stuff like this is that Apple might like the way BioTelemetry's devices and software work with its watch and might decide to buy the company outright instead of developing additional services for its Watch in house. Buyouts like this though don't happen often and the stock should not be bought for that reason alone in my opinion. Rather, look at the fundamentals, the partnership, and the growth into a new area of monitoring in clinical situations for reasons to buy into a company like this.

4. *Betting on a turnaround story.* These stories have been some of the harder lessons to learn as catching a falling knife means a high likelihood of getting cut in the process along the way that a could take years to appear. Not only do you have to wait for the fundamental issues to start to look better for the company, you also have to figure out when market sentiment will start shifting again in the company's favor. I find the best way to play these types of stocks is

to buy in at half positions throughout the year gradually building a position up in the stock. A lot of times the stock still has additional downside left in it, which means you can average down easily getting a better average share price in a stock you still believe in, or you can easily get out if your sentiment towards the stock and situation change since you first bought in.

One of my favorite stories that fits under this category has been the former Valeant Pharmaceuticals, now Bausch Health Companies Inc. (BHC) of course, after its precipitous fall from about $258 a share in 2015 to around $9 a share by 2017. Most of these losses came pretty quickly as price gouging and fraud issues, along with a huge turn in sentiment based on the company's massive debt load from prior acquisitions, caused a run on the stock as the public, along with politically powerful spokespeople, picked it up as a poster child for what is wrong with drug prices and the health care system as a whole. This wave of heavy and sustained headwinds were exacerbated by the company's strategy of using debt to buy other companies for rapid expansion of growth and cash flows while sustaining an ever ballooning debt balance of over $30 billion dollars. Debt is fine and dandy when you are a growing company with good prospects, but as soon as the vultures start to circle, it can be the anchor that drops you to the bottom of the ocean.

I picked up the stock and started writing about Valeant while it was still named Valeant Pharmaceuticals in the $20's, as by then it had a new CEO in place with what I believed was a very solid and doable stabilization plan after listening to his shareholder meeting. He planned to stop the bloodshed by selling off non-core assets, fixing the company's credibility image, proactively paying down the company's debt load as quickly as possible, all while bringing growth back to the company's core assets including its Bausch and Lomb division along with its newly acquired Salix business. It was a good plan and has had remarkable results to date, but market sentiment can be very slow to shift and change in turnaround stories, especially when a heavy debt load is involved.

Valeant's CEO Joe Papa has paid the company's debt down from a high of around $32 billion to around $25 billion in a short time while maintaining and turning around a lot of the company's core assets after sales had been dropping across the board for the company. However, the stock dropped all the way into the high single digits before bottoming out, and has recovered now into the mid $20's. It is a longer and slower process than many would think and the best way to play it was to buy in small amounts over an extended time period until a clear bottom has formed with hopefully a purchase around that low mark. I still maintain my position in the stock, as a long term holding, because I still see plenty of upside in the coming years as the company continues to execute marvelously. However, I am fully aware that it will take a long time for the market to fully come around on the company again after at least a few years in the doghouse.

Its lots of fun to make some speculative bets over the year on stocks but try to keep the bets respectable and be prepared to lose or win big as events unfold. Always have your core base of great stocks and funds to rely on over the year with speculation bets making up a small portion of your total assets.

Chapter 11
The Communications Services Sector

Giving From Your Heart And Soul Is Hard, But The Rewards Can Be Immeasurable.
- Author

"As We Look Ahead Into The Next Century, Leaders Will Be Those Who Empower Others."
- Bill Gates

    The Communications Services Sector was a smaller part of my portfolio at the beginning of 2018, when it was the former Telecommunications Sector, mostly based around dividend producing players along with occasional bets on some growth or consolidation names. I used to keep this sector around 5% of my portfolio and mainly tried to grow my core holdings in this sector around the dividends and growth prospects that appealed to me at that particular time. However, in September of 2018, this sector completely changed with the addition of many new intriguing new stocks that resulted in me changing my target allocation for this sector from 5% of my portfolio all the way up to 15% of my portfolio. The main sector ETF representing the new Communications Services Sector I plan to use going forward is the (XLC).

This sector is becoming more and more interesting to me with the rapid rise of 5G, which might result in a new technology revolution led by some of the more traditional big players in the sector. The rapid rise of 5G might make companies like AT&T Inc. (T) and Verizon Communications (VZ) a little more appealing along with key additions to the sector of investor favorites like Facebook (FB), Netflix (NFLX), and Google-owner Alphabet (GOOGL).

I will let the new Communications Services Sector changes settle in for a few months along with watching the development of 5G over the back half of 2018. When 2019 comes around, I plan on fully reconfiguring my portfolio to reflect the newly revamped Communications Services Sector as I make plans for 2019's IRA and potential 401k deposits. I'll make small changes along the way to try and get my allocations in line with my new expectations with bigger changes coming at the end of the year after the dust of the changes has settled. At that time I also will be doing some general buying and selling from stocks and sectors that have run over the past year into sectors that I think are lagging where I want them to be. I'm thinking the beginning of 2019 will be a big rebalancing year for me as sector changes don't come around too often, and present a great opportunity to re-evaluate everything and clean house and start the year with a freshly balanced portfolio after I mark all the changes to the stocks I love to follow and own.

The easiest way to play this sector now and in the future is just to use the corresponding sector ETF, which is the (XLC), unless you know off hand which of the major telecom players currently best fits your long-term strategy to pair with the newer growth based FANG stocks that now help dominate the sector. My strategy is to find the telecom provider I like the best at this time and slowly build that position over time while adding to my FANG plays to get my sector position up near the 15% that I am currently desiring at this time. With the rise of 5G and the acquisition of the former Time Warner Inc. (TWX), I actually ended up liquidating my former Verizon Communications (VZ) position in favor of the higher dividend and 5G leader, AT&T Inc. (T).

A good starting point for many newer investors with a long time horizon is in some of the FANG stocks popularized by Jim Cramer, the host of Mad Money, that are the core stocks shaping and defining our world as we know it at this time. The FANG acronym for the stocks Facebook (FB), Amazon (AMZN), Netflix (NFLX), and Google (GOOG or GOOGL) (who's parent company is Alphabet) is fun to say and encompasses a lot of the main trendy Communications Services stocks of the day excluding Amazon Inc. which still resides in the Consumer Discretionary Sector. As these stocks have grown and changed the world, some have moved to other sectors of the market even though many investors would initially think of them as purely technology stocks.

Here is a general comparison of some of the metrics for FAANG (includes Apple Inc. (AAPL) stocks to use when comparing them as many investors will want to make bets on at least a couple of the stocks in their portfolio, or instead have some decent exposure to a broader ranged ETF like (FNG) from AdvisorShares which encompasses 28 "disruptive innovators" that fit the FANG model. Figuring out which of the FAANG names you like best and want to invest in will help you set up your investing goals for each sector means they can be such a moving force, especially now in the newly created Communications Services Sector.

FAANG	Market Cap	P/E	Forward P/E	PEG	Dividend Yield
Facebook	$379B	17.78	17.84	0.99	NA
Amazon	$734B	92.34	NA	2.68	NA
Apple	$675B	11.71	11.44	0.90	2.05%
Netflix	$118B	93.71	101.84	1.64	NA
Google	$355B	25.18	24.54	1.52	NA

Table by Trent Welsh

    One way the Communications Services Sector might grow and change is by how a company like Netflix (NFLX) can come to dominate and expand into media companies and their corresponding actions. Think if Netflix continued to grow its content of movies and shows by buying a media company like Lions Gate Entertainment Corp. (LGF.A) (LGF.B) or merged with a giant like Disney (DIS). Also, what if Netflix decided to go after news stations or sports stations and bought a company like Twenty-First Century Fox's (FOXA) (FOX) news division or a cable company like Charter Communications Inc. (CHTR) for example. Regulatory issues might abound for a company like Netflix, which is on the cutting edge of the new media landscape, which is possibly why it is not a player in some of the most recent M&A drama, but instead spends billions of dollars a year developing its own content. This has not hampered Netflix at all from surpassing Disney's market cap though, which is truly astounding when you consider how fast Netflix has risen, and how great a company Disney still continues to be.

Disney and Comcast bid for Fox Deal Case

M&A has been so fierce and potentially lucrative in the sector recently that I ended up actually selling my core Walt Disney Company (DIS) stock position in my portfolio in December of 2017, which I had formerly planned on holding until retirement. I did this because Disney had just agreed to purchase the bulk of Twenty-First Century Fox's (FOXA) (FOX) assets in an all-stock deal. After the deal closed, Fox's shareholders would get Disney stock back in return, along with stock in a newly created "NewFox" company with the assets in it that regulators wouldn't allow Disney to keep in the deal like Fox's news network means Disney already owns ABC. Regulators would never go for the same company having more than one major news outlet along with Disney owning assets like ESPN along with all of Fox's regional sports networks.

I love deals like this, so I sold my original Disney shares and bought Fox shares with the understanding that I would get Disney shares back again in a year or two, after regulators did their analysis, along with the bonus NewFox shares which analysts initially thought might be worth around $10 a share. What I did not count on was that later on around the summer of 2018, AT&T Inc. (T) won a two-year-long drawn out battle against regulators for its acquisition of Time Warner Inc. (TWX) in what ended up a very embarrassing case for the Justice Department.

Emboldened by this regulatory win, Comcast Corporation (CMCSA) decided to make a formal bid for Fox's assets even though the Disney and Fox deal was already almost 6 months into the regulatory process. This has resulted in an escalating bidding war between Comcast and Disney for Fox, which has driven Fox's share price up dramatically from where it traded even after the Disney and Fox deal was originally sealed. I have used the opportunity to repeatedly up my holdings in Fox over the year so that now, with the additional buys along with the remarkable share appreciation, Fox has become a giant holding in my portfolio where it will likely stay for another year or so while bids and regulatory issues finish up.

I love M&A deals like this because there is limited downside risk because especially in all-cash deals, the shareholders will get the same cash at the deal closing regardless if the market gained 50% over the past year or lost 50% of its value. Also, with an all-stock deal like Disney's original offer, Fox's shareholders will still end up with Disney stock at the end of the day even if the market has a horrible year. Sure Disney stock will be down, but great company's can survive downturns in the market better than many smaller more speculative company.

At the end of the day, Disney should win the bidding war for Fox's assets after regulatory approvals some time in 2019, and think I will possibly take half of my holdings in Disney stock and half in cash along with shares of NewFox when the deal closes. Even if Comcast had finished up as the winner for most of Fox's assets, my plan would have been most likely to sell Fox's shares then and use the proceeds to buy Disney stock again, with the profits all going towards other new investments. I have had some great luck with M&A deals in the past and continue to look for two to three good deals a year to bet on as I love many of the complex results from these agreements over time.

As I mentioned before, one of the biggest upcoming issues for this sector is the expected rise of 5G, which is currently rolling out in 2018, with a more rapid expansion planned in 2019 and 2020. Of course all the major players will have their hands in the honey pot for this one but certain companies should have certain advantages compared to other players in the space. Some of the earliest movers and best positioned to benefit from the rise of 5G are AT&T Inc. (T) and Verizon Communications (VZ).

Players like Sprint Corporation (S) has an abundance of spectrum, which might help to give it an advantage when 5G becomes more widespread, but it should be far more concerned about passing regulators concerning its scheduled upcoming merger with T-Mobile US, Inc. (TMUS). This potential merger will take major US carriers down to 3 players from the current 4 so it most likely will have a bumpy and long regulator ride even with AT&T's (T) recent win over regulators in acquiring the former Time Warner Inc. (TWX).

A successful merger of T-Mobile and Sprint should help these laggards for into another potential leader in 5G and future technologies with potentially more spectrum than AT&T and Verizon. Sprint's parent company SoftBank Group ADR (SFTBY) holds over 80% of Sprint's (S) shares and has been actively looking for a partner for Sprint now for the last couple years before finally getting a potential deal done with T-Mobile (TMUS). While these merger talks and plans have failed in the past, Softbank's CEO Masayoshi Son is a very dedicated individual who believes in his ability to get a deal done and past regulators. He is also smart enough to have a potential backup plan or two in place as he has shown some of his intent by having Softbank quietly acquire a little over 5% of Charter Communications Inc.'s (CHTR) shares at the beginning of 2018.

Here are some of the core stocks currently in the Telecommunications Services Sector that I have liked better than other stocks in this smaller section of my portfolio, at least for now. They include AT&T Inc. (T), Verizon Communications (VZ), T-Mobile US Inc. (TMUS), Sprint Corporation (S), and Charter Communications Inc. (CHTR).

Telecom	Market Cap	P/E	Forward P/E	PEG	Dividend Yield
AT&T	$215B	14.748	8.41	2.51	6.90%
Verizon	$232B	15.00	12.05	2.80	4.29%
T-Mobile	$55B	20.34	19.62	NA	NA
Sprint	$25B	54.08	103.3	NA	NA
Charter	$66B	50.85	52.36	0.87	NA

Table by Trent Welsh

As far as value plays currently for the space, I have not considered many names besides one of my favorite conglomerates in SoftBank Group ADR (SFTBY). This conglomerate is based in Japan, I love the international diversification exposure here, which was based originally on a leading Japanese telecommunications company. It has grown into owning many other investments including most of Sprint, along with a sizeable holding in another stock I love Alibaba Group Holding Limited (BABA). Alibaba is a stock that I love to own by proxy which means that I have never traded Alibaba itself, but I have loved looking at and owning both Altaba Inc. (AABA) and

SoftBank instead, both of which own oodles of Alibaba shares along with their other assets.

Value	Market Cap	P/E	Forward P/E	PEG	Dividend Yield
SoftBank	$95.6B	10.37	NA	NA	0.53%

Table by Trent Welsh

SoftBank Case

SoftBank Group ADR (SFTBY) is one of the more interesting conglomerates in the market in my mind, as it has some made some tremendous bets in the past that have created monumental shareholder value. It also continues to have an eye towards the future as it has built its $100 billion dollar Vision Fund to invest in public and private companies that are looking to change the face of the future.

Here are some of the main holdings the company has made in the past which have reaped some tremendous benefits for shareholders, especially with the rise of Alibaba.

| SoftBank | Domestic Telco | Sprint | Alibaba | ARM | Yahoo Japan |

Table by Trent Welsh

As far as SoftBank's Vision Fund goes, here are some of the investments the fund has already made in companies that could very well help define key growth areas of the future. This $100 billion fund was originally seeded by SoftBank, with $25 billion of its own money, while it started looking for partners. It caught the interest of some major investors along the way with up to $45 billion of Saudi Arabia's public investment fund now a part of the Vision Fund. Here's a look at some of the companies the Vision Fund has already invested in.

Slide from Q3, 2018 Earnings Call

Here's a quote from SoftBank's CEO Masayoshi Son on his $100 billion dollar Vision Fund:

"Technology has the potential to address the biggest challenges and risks facing humanity today. The businesses working to solve these problems will require patient long-term capital and visionary strategic investment partners with the resources to nurture their success. SoftBank has long made bold investments in transformative technologies and supported disruptive entrepreneurs. The SoftBank Vision Fund is consistent with this strategy and will help build and grow businesses creating the foundational platforms of the next stage of the Information Revolution."

Quote from SoftBank's webpage
https://softbank-ia.com/vision-fund.

Considering the success Son has had in investing in great companies like Alibaba and Sprint in the past, I find SoftBank a compelling stock to own for the long-haul as its investments might take years to pay off, but might pay off in a huge way for investors.

I have mostly stayed away from speculation stocks in this sector, as it has traditionally been a small part of my portfolio in the past, mainly with a big U.S. telecom giant or two for the sake of diversity. A couple stocks I have followed and considered before, but never have officially pulled the trigger on, are Alibaba Group ADR (BABA) along with Frontier Communications Corporation (FTR) which has fallen like a rock for years resulting in a pretty ridiculous dividend return. A lot of times, when dividends are too good to be believed, they are on the verge of being cut or even eliminated by that troubled company. However, especially around ex-dividend days, I have considered trading the Frontier stock. I have never been able to pull the trigger on it though as I always figure the day after the dividend gets locked in is most likely a day where the stock finds a way to explore a new low.

Alibaba I put into the speculative category in the past primarily because it was a Chinese company with its IPO only a couple years ago. It is listed on a U.S exchange though and has a lot more transparency than most Chinese companies. I plan on moving this company up to a more core position soon as its earnings and performance have solidified and the company now as one of the most predictable and reliable among the Chinese stocks. When I shift around my views of all the sectors in early 2019, after September's new Communications Services Sector formation, Alibaba will officially graduate from speculation to a potential core main holding for my portfolio. I continue to especially love it, as it adds to my international exposure, but will continue to own it by proxy by investing in SoftBank and Altaba Inc. (AABA) most likely in the future as well.

Speculative	Market Cap	P/E	Forward P/E	PEG	Dividend Yield
Alibaba	$339B	38.98	25.13	1.54	NA
Frontier	$247M	NA	NA	NA	NA

Table by Trent Welsh

Chapter 12
The Materials Sector

Buy A Stock A Year, Write A Page A Day, Start Today For Big Results Tomorrow.
- Author

"Be The Change That You Wish To See In The World."
- Mahatma Gandhi

The Materials Sector always feels like a more unloved sector of the market where I have a lot more interest than most regular investors. The basic building blocks of the market are subject to regular supply and demand cycles, which come and go with global growth and slowdowns, along with logistical issues from global deposits. This sector should compromise maybe up to about 6% of your portfolio with a good mix of dividend producers along with some growth names. As you age though, it potentially could become a bigger part of your portfolio as you add more defensive names to your portfolio holdings including more bonds and basic material stocks based on gold, silver, or even sand.

The ETF for the sector is the XLB for basic materials and includes everything from gold and silver to uranium, copper, sand, and feature stocks holding the materials as well as mining companies specializing in those specific materials. The chemical industry is also in this sector as they are the building blocks of material goods like plastics across the globe.

Gold and other precious metals should offer a limited hedge for investors as a lot of times they are seen as a "safe" play in a crashing market where investors put their assets when it seems like all stocks are falling to pieces. Gold is a nice simple asset to own that most investors understand and can be easily traded at any time in stock form or physical form. However, I think attitudes have changed over time in regard to gold in that it might not be quite the safe play that it used to be. Its hard to say now how gold will react to an extended downturn or recession, especially now with additional "commodity" like products like Bitcoin and Etherium in the market. Many investors now view Bitcoin as something similar to gold except that it is stored in a digital wallet instead of in a bank vault for physical gold.

When you are ready to decide on investing in a particular precious metal or two, figure out if you want to own the physical metal itself like gold and silver coins, or the stocks of companies that hold gold reserves in a bank vault somewhere based on inflows and outflows of cash into the security, which physically backs the value of the stocks, or finally, if you want to own a mining company itself that mines the physical metal you are interested in itself. The main difference is the level of safety you want compared to the level of potential growth you would desire.

If you own physical gold, your returns will primarily depend on whether the intrinsic value of gold any given day is trending higher or lower. However, if you own a gold miner in Africa, your returns might vary considerably not only with the volatility of gold itself, but on whether the mining company is having success in making any new discoveries to replenish the current mines it operates. You also have to keep an eye on the political stability of the country the mine is in along with taxes and worker concerns including work halts, revolutions, and mining accidents or disasters. Of course, if your mining company discovers a large deposit of gold that can be mined at a very reasonable cost, your stock might see some rapid price appreciation in a very short time period regardless of how the value of gold itself is trending.

Physically owning precious metals usually is in the form of owning some gold and precious stone jewelry like diamonds along with maybe some physical coins or bars that are kept in coin books in the family safe at home or in a bank vault. Storage costs for most people usually are minimal means most people have some sort of jewelry, even if it's mostly custom or cheap jewelry, along with a jewelry box, chest, small safe, or a hidden place under the mattress to keep it in. Even buying a roll of silver or gold coins a year wouldn't be that big of a storage issue for most people, especially if you have a bank close by that rents out small deposit boxes which can easily hold quite a few rolls of coins.

Stocks that are associated with their own vault and reserves are interesting because you can feel like you physically own the precious metal inside without having to deal with the actual storage and insurance issue. Theoretically, when a million dollars comes in to this type of stock or fund, they go out and buy a million dollars worth of the metal it tracks and put it in the vault, and when a million dollars gets redeemed by an investor, they go and sell a million dollars worth of the metal to reflect the redemption. This means that the stock has to have a cash buffer though, that is not invested directly in metal assets to facilitate quick trades, which earns minimal interest along with the frequent trading in the metal, which all goes into the overall expenses of owning the stock or fund.

Also, consider if there is a market crash in the metal and all the fund's investors want an immediate redemption. This might create a halt in the stock meaning that most investors won't get to cash out quickly means it takes time to sell the metal, which potentially means that the investors at the end of the line are left with virtually nothing if the material ends up virtually worthless. That is also why a lot of funds have waiting periods for large redemption orders or limits and restrictions on redemptions to help keep a panic from bankrupting the fund overnight. These types of stocks are some of my least favorite in the sector as I am fine with limited coins and jewelry for physically owning some precious metals along with more growth orientated mining stocks.

One of the main concern with mining stocks is the physical location where the mines are. For example, many of the best gold or diamond mines are located in areas of the world that are potentially less stable than other areas of the world at any given time. Regulations, taxes, and labor laws vary widely and can depend heavily on whether a mine is located in North America compared to if one is in Africa or Australia. Also, consider that political and social instability in different countries, even some of the most stable countries, can ebb and flow resulting in mine closures or worker walkouts that can devastate the cash flows of a mining company in the short-term that is primarily focused on one area of the world. With the increased risks, come increased rewards as many of these companies are continually looking for additional reserves to replace mines in use that have a limited life until they are abandoned. Mining stocks also can sport terrific dividends especially if mining prices are appreciating and the costs of metal retrieval are stable or even falling at the company's mines.

Here are some of my favorite bigger name materials stocks featuring the mining company Barrick Gold Corp. (GOLD), the SPDR Gold Trust ETF (GLD), Applied Materials (AMAT), and DowDuPont Inc. (DWDP) for chemicals.

Materials	Market Cap	P/E	Forward P/E	PEG	Dividend Yield
Barrick	$15.2B	NA	31.18	NA	2.15%
GLD	NA	NA	NA	NA	NA
Applied Materials	$30B	7.32	9.27	0.43	2.54%
Dow DuPont	$121B	112.25	12.76	16.04	2.89%

Table by Trent Welsh

    For a core holding or two I would pick out a main metal of choice from gold, silver, aluminum, copper, uranium or whatever rare earth metal is currently in vogue for future technology and pair it with a chemicals company for some nice diversification to start in the sector. Feel free to count any physical coins or jewelry that you own initially in your calculations, to help you get diversified quicker, so that you don't overload your holdings all into gold when it might be a better idea to have some gold along with a copper stock, or to buy DuPont instead of the GLD ETF when you just bought a couple of expensive gold coins on eBay Inc. (EBAY) for your home safe.

Value plays in the sector are more often composed of the less exciting materials in the space that are common and often follow demand and supply cycles as global growth accelerates or slows down. It's a lot less exciting initially to be invested in aluminum than gold, but I have always had more exposure to aluminum than to gold over my investing career means I went more for value when I initially started buying into the sector.

Gold is precious, and thus more exciting to most investors, but I find it interesting to follow how aluminum is faring in the real world as its alloys continue to replace steel in lighter weight automobiles, and superior forms of it are used in aircraft parts, defense, and space exploration. Materials don't have to be exotic to be valuable and even the most common stuff like sand can make you returns above and beyond what precious gold can accomplish if your timing and research are good. Here are some of the more "boring" value plays in the sector that I have traded over the past, with my personal favorite being aluminum. They include Alcoa Corp (AA), Freeport-McMoRan Inc. (FCX), Rio Tinto plc (RIO), and Vulcan Materials Company (VMC)

Value	Market Cap	P/E	Forward P/E	PEG	Dividend Yield
Alcoa	$4.9B	917	7.24	229	NA
Freeport-McMoRan	$15B	5.33	6.14	1.01	1.99%
Rio Tinto	$60B	8.05	9.24	NA	6.60%
Vulcan Materials	$13B	30.49	24.38	1.18	1.16%

Table by Trent Welsh

As far as speculative plays go in the materials sector, some of my favorites are in the booming American energy market including frac sand producers like Hi-Crush Partners LP (HCLP).

Hi-Crush Case

Hi-Crush Partners LP (HCLP) had a marvelous run during America's energy boom in 2014 as a frac sand provider with its stock heading from around $20 a unit to almost $70 a unit in about a year as oil crossed over $100 a barrel. Then came the crash from global oversupply, which sent oil down into the $20-$30 a barrel range which resulted in a similar crash in Hi-

Crush's stock down into the single digits. This resulted in sand mines, oil rigs, and production plants being shut down across the U.S. as oil had suddenly become unprofitable for just about everyone in the business except for ultra low cost producers.

While oil companies and their suppliers went through a rough patch along with investors for a few years, those companies that survived learned to survive by taking a lot of costs out of their business models. They also focused on implementing new technologies and materials, along with new frac sand techniques, that allowed for even cheaper ways to get oil and gas out of the ground than was ever possible before. The cost of retrieving oil out of the Permian Basin using frac sand was pretty much halved over this time period, from shipping it in from sources in Wisconsin at about $110 per ton, to having plants set up in and around the Permian Basin that can truck in frac sand to the oil well sites quickly and far more efficiently.

The first company to get a Kermit plant up and running in the Permian Basin was Hi-Crush. It can now supply some of the lowest cost sand to oil production sites across the basin, that continue to use more and more sand per rig to get their oil more efficiently out of the ground as frac techniques continue to evolve. Hi-

Crush also owns a lot of the train terminals that it uses to ship sand to the Permian and other Basins across the U.S. from sources in Wisconsin, which gives it a competitive advantage over much of the competition in that area as well. Finally, Hi-Crush has a phenomenal last mile service option for its customers that gets the sand from Hi-Crush's Kermit plant all the way to the well site and into the ground using Hi-Crush employees, trucks, and equipment all for a small upcharge to the customer.

    Here is a look at how Hi-Crush has been performing over the past couple of quarters even as its stock price remains depressed as oil prices continue to trend higher after its recent fall from grace after its 2014 highs.

Hi-Crush	Q3/17	Q4/17	Growth
Revenues	$167.6M	$216.5M	29.2%
Sand Prices (Per Ton)	$68	$71	4.4%
Sand Volumes (Tons)	2,456,195	2,985,115	21.5%
Contribution Margin	$19.39	$23.46	21%
Distribution	$0.15	$0.20	33.3%
Distributive Cash Flow	$37.5M	$52.6M	40.3%

Table by Trent Welsh

With numbers like this, along with oil trading profitably above $50, $60, $70, and even potentially higher a barrel, it should only be a matter of time before sentiment turns around on stocks like. Hi-Crush and other companies in the sector are making money hand-over-fist over the short-term, and yet their stocks trade at deep discounts because of market fears of another crash in oil prices and incoming supply concerns in the sector during the U.S. energy boom.

Of course, maybe sentiment is right to continue being negative and another oil crash is right around the corner after half a dozen other companies set up shop in the Permian Basin and across the U.S. That is why I trade in and out of the stock by taking profits along the way while trying to always maintain a long position in this stock. Buy into an oversized position when the stock has had a nice 20%-30% short-term drop, and sell into a small or regular position after it starts reaching new 52-week highs. It's a cyclical speculative stock so it makes sense to me to trade it with additional buying and selling, compared to my regular core holdings, as it continues its high volatility roller coaster ride over the year.

I am not betting the farm on it or any other stock, and will be able to let it go if supply and oil pricing do become a huge concern again, but my profits along the way over the past year will pretty much guarantee that I'll end up a winner at the end of the day with this speculative stock. There are always opportunities and values out there in every sector of the market, so spread out your risk and take many bets you think are potential big winners instead of putting all of your eggs into just a few small baskets.

Although Hi-Crush is not the biggest frac sand producing company out there, it is definitely one of the best at what it does at this time. I like a lot of things the company is currently doing and think that Hi-Crush has a at least a few great years of production coming up as the U.S. emerges as a global powerhouse in fossil fuel production.

Chapter 13
The Consumer Discretionary Sector

Jump, Ask Directions Along The Way.
- Author

"It Is Amazing What You Can Accomplish If You Do Not Care Who Gets The Credit."
- Harry S. Truman

The Consumer Discretionary Sector was a smaller portion of my portfolio for quite awhile until the beginning of 2018, when it grew very quickly into a surprisingly big section of my portfolio with the advent of some heavy hitting M&A action in the sector including stocks like the Walt Disney Company (DIS) and Twenty-First Century Fox (FOX) (FOXA). It remained a bigger portion of my portfolio until the back end of 2018 when Disney and Fox stocks moved to the newly renamed and revamped Communications Services Sector. There have been a lot of changes to this sector over the course of the year in my portfolio, which means this is one of the core sectors I will reevaluate in

2019 after all the changes have settled. Currently I am looking for a 6% target for the sector in my total portfolio as several of the key names I loved most in the sector left in the September 2018 sector shift.

I plan on refocusing again a little bit more on high dividends in this sector along with the amazing potential growth in the sector of a few key companies like Amazon.com (AMZN). Most of the positions I started in the past in this sector were small ones that were easy to trade out of if I needed some quick funds for a new buying opportunity. As my retirement portfolio grows and expands, I plan on settling more into a few main stocks to focus on instead of half a dozen small positions across the sector. For now though, I mainly hold a few small positions in different areas of the sector, along with my core mutual fund and index holdings.

First, things might be changing in the future as technology giants like Amazon.com (AMZN) continue to aggressively expand their horizons by entering new sectors of the market with immediate affects on all other participants in that sector. Although Amazon is technically in the Consumer Discretionary Sector, quite a few at home investors would automatically think of it as a technology stock and lump it in with their technology holdings for how they allocate funds. Be careful in figuring out which sectors stocks like this go as companies that can return 100%-1000% in a matter of years can quickly throw your portfolio out of whack, especially if you consider it as part of another sector of your portfolio entirely.

One example on how Amazon is changing the world is Amazon's latest purchase of Whole Foods, bringing the previous online company into the brick-and-mortar retail segment it was never a part of before. If Amazon continues to grow its retail brick-and-mortar exposure, might it even eventually more logically trade in the Consumer Staples Sector of the market if it truly becomes a staple of almost every household in America whether offline or online? This retail dominance is a possibility as its technology could define a new futuristic grocery store experience that might include no lines or cashiers.

Amazon's technology could track your purchases as you walk around the store, through video surveillance along with sensors in grocery carts, and would automatically check you out and charge your account as you walk through the door with your items without even the need to talk to or see another employee. This pretty amazing future technology is on our doorstep, so how do you classify a technology company that now dominates online retail and now wants to compete directly with giants like Wal-Mart (WMT) and Kroger (KR) potentially years from now in brick-and-mortar retail. Consumer's tastes and preferences are always changing which makes this sector of the market potentially very interesting as it has more than a few companies in it that can and are changing the world in ways we could only barely imagine a handful of years ago.

With rapid up and coming companies like Amazon (AMZN) dominating growth and reactive M&A activity in the Consumer Discretionary Sector, might it be getting too big and powerful in achieving an almost monopoly like position in the market? Amazon might be getting big and fearsome so fast that they might start drawing additional scrutiny from government officials and legislators like Microsoft (MSFT) did in the 1990's as a monopoly concern due for a possible breakup. Just something to keep in mind as Amazon continues to dominate every space it touches.

I think that with the growth and pace of domination of a handful of companies over the past decade, the government might have no choice but to step in and break up a company like Amazon into pieces even though it dominates in many different businesses with plenty of competition in each different business. It is very hard to say if and when the government might want to step in and where a line might be drawn, but it is something to be aware of because it took Microsoft quite a while to recover from government intervention in the 90's due to monopoly concerns.

This Consumer Discretionary Sector is an amazing sector in my mind as it also contains automobiles, hotels, casinos, and restaurants along with traditional retail players. With such a diverse array of stocks in this sector from the super high growth, to the big dividend automobile stocks, to the beaten down retail segment that has been beaten down tremendously over the past few years thanks to players like Amazon.com (AMZN), investors should have no trouble picking out some winners they love. The retail giants that can survive the Amazon scare over time should be pretty attractive buys at low valuations once the industry finishes pushing out the unneeded excess retail baggage, and the remaining players consolidate into a few bigger more specialized names. Beware also the smaller players though who don't have a specialized niche, that can be inadvertently forced out of the market as there currently is just too much brick-and-mortar retail space in the market. Only those retail players that can ultimately change and adapt to keep up with Amazon.com (AMZN), and the ever-evolving picky consumer, can hope to reap the rewards of surviving the lightning fast shift in consumer spending practices.

After initial mutual funds and index funds, an investor might be interested in the general sector ETF the (XLY), or you might just want to dive in with a core holding of a brand that you are especially fond of for whatever reason. In the past I was leery of the sector because of the havoc Amazon was wrecking along with the fact that a few years ago I couldn't bring myself to buy Amazon stock because I kept telling myself it was way too expensive given its P/E value. This is why I initially kept my exposure small with an assortment of smaller holdings in the sector. As consumer preferences seem to be constantly changing, I didn't want to be left out in the rain on a stock that was ultimately left for dead when consumers changed their attitudes, and decided to spend their dollars on a new product now in vogue.

However, my old beliefs have changed considerably as I have watched Amazon grow and dominate not only online retail, but other areas as well, including cloud computing and its array of products for

Amazon Prime. I now fully understand why Amazon requires such an extravagant P/E value, which is why I have started trying to accumulate a share here or there over time as I now aim to make a couple small Amazon stock purchases a year now that I have become a full believer in the story.

Here are some of the core names that I have considered and owned in the past that I think might have some moats that hopefully can withstand the changing times, or even companies like Amazon.com (AMZN), the electric vehicle revolution led by companies like Tesla Motors (TSLA), or even private companies like Airbnb.com that are looking to disrupt the hotel industry. There is so much disruption and upheaval going on now around the bigger stocks in this sector that I try to keep my exposure low in many of the names I hold until it becomes more clear who the ultimate winners and losers are. Some of my plays in this sector have included core names like Nike Inc. (NKE), Ford Motor Company (F), General Motors Company (GM), Las Vegas Sands Corp. (LVS), and Amazon.com (AMZN).

Consumer Discretionary	Market Cap	P/E	Forward P/E	PEG	Dividend Yield
Nike	$116B	28.31	27.62	2.00	1.21%
Ford	$31B	5.36	5.84	0.36	7.71%
General Motors	$46B	5.48	5.13	0.38	4.71%
Las Vegas Sands	$41B	15.88	15.41	2.38	5.74%
Amazon	$734B	92.34	NA	2.68	NA

Table by Trent Welsh

Notice the nice dividends that the automobile companies are sporting? I love buying into Ford (F) especially when I feel I don't have a great stock name to put extra money into at that time for any number of reasons. I use Ford as a type of holding stock a lot of times, because the volatility in the stock is pretty low and its dividend is usually around 5%, which is a great quarterly reward as I hold Ford until I see something I love then I can easily sell it and buy into the new opportunity.

Ford isn't revolutionizing the car market, but it also won't be going bankrupt any time soon. It showed its durability when back in 2009-2013 the Big Three automakers, Ford (F) General Motors Company (GM), and the now Fiat Chrysler Automobiles NV (FCAU) went before Congress warning of bankruptcy and the loss of one million jobs unless they got bailed out by the U.S. tax payer. Ford had already cut costs substantially by this time so it didn't need the bailout, it just didn't want to get left behind if the government gave a free ride to the other U.S. car giants.

As far as value plays go in the sector, I would say hit up some of the best retail names in the sector that are still trading at depressed numbers from fears of Amazon.com (AMZN) driving all retail out of business. There are a lot of very profitable names out there that have come a long ways over the years in catching up to Amazon's online lead with their own digital initiatives and customer perks like curbside pickup and free or cheap two day delivery also. Some names that fit a good value in my mind are names like Macy's Inc. (M), Target Corporation (TGT), Tractor Supply Company (TSCO) and Nordstrom Inc. (JWN). Nordstrom is especially interesting because its founding family has tried unsuccessfully in the recent past to take the company private again. So you get the mostly cheap valuation, along with a possible takeover scenario again in due time, which I often find irresistible for a small bet now and then on these types of stocks.

Values	Market Cap	P/E	Forward P/E	PEG	Dividend Yield
Macy's	$9B	8.19	7.03	NA	5.07%
Target	$34B	12.58	12.15	1.57	3.91%
Tractor Supply	$10B	19.58	18.85	1.35	1.54%
Nordstrom	$8B	15.87	13.05	1.69	3.15%

Table by Trent Welsh

Tractor Supply Company Case

One of my favorite traditional plays in the value space in consumer discretionary though has to be Tractor Supply Company (TSCO), which I believe has some inherent defenses against the Amazon (AMZN) death star along with ever-elusive growth. This moat against Amazon is because a lot of Tractor Supply's sales come from bulky items and equipment such as of course tractors, fencing, and other items that are difficult to sell on websites such as Amazon.com. It also has its own rural niche market of dedicated and loyal customers who might find it harder to switch to a competitor than if Tractor Supply was just another clothing store in the mall for instance.

It also has jumped on the pet care growth bandwagon with its recent acquisition of PetSense stores. This gives the company the ability to use a greater part of their retail store footprint for value enhancing pet sales, with differentiated and distinct brands, along with developing their own private label brands built around the core PetSense brands. The attractive margins, in this fast growing part of the market, look like they will help boost profitability for years to come for Tractor Supply.

The company is also rapidly growing standalone PetSense stores that might make terrific small store concepts in key urban areas and markets where a full Tractor Supply store might not make sense. This will help the company break into new markets for new customers along with getting the information and data they need to determine if expansion in the area with additional PetSense stores or maybe a full Tractor Supply store makes sense for the future growth of the company.

Tractor Supply is a well-run specialty retailer with a natural moat against Amazon, growth in its traditional stores, growth in its PetSense stores, and an eye on digital initiatives like new enhanced online ordering and in-store pickup policies that will help make shopping even more convenient for its customers. The best part is that this company often trades at a terrific value as it usually gets lumped in with traditional retail, which continues to get its lunch money stolen from Amazon.

As far as speculative stocks go for this sector, I tend to stay away from most names in this area, as a lot of the beaten down names are retail names that look like they might be exploring bankruptcies like a Sears Holdings Corporation (SHLDQ) for example. Otherwise maybe for fast growing companies like a Tesla Inc. (TSLA), which many might consider in the Technology sector, but is actually a part of the beaten down automotive sector in Consumer Discretionary. I am a fan of trading Tesla on big dips, but have not taken it on as a core position, because I think one day it will trade with the other autos which might mean a big drop in share price eventually if and when the other auto companies catch up to electric and autonomous driving. Of course, maybe Tesla continues to shape and define automobiles, batteries, and solar initiatives for the next decade making its current high P/E valuation well worth the price for years to come.

Another speculative stock like the former rock star company turned dog recently in a company like Under Armour (UA) (UAA), which I have liked in the past, and now trades at a lot better valuation than it did when I first bought shares in the company. It justified its high P/E valuation for years with phenomenal growth before its growth rate eventually slowed, especially in North America along with most other apparel producers in the U.S. This slow down resulted in the stock dropping by about 75%, making it a much more attractive and safer buy now as it still is a fine company in my eyes and a lot more fairly valued.

Finally, maybe a hot growth name in the restaurant sector that has had tremendous returns for years, but has been taken to the woodshed by the market for health concerns a couple of times now in Chipotle Mexican Grill, Inc. (CMG). Chipotle traded at half the value it did a mere couple of years ago and seems to have gotten its act together as the stock finally made a comeback. The vote is still out on whether it can maintain its mojo and massive growth with dedicated followers, or if that day is fading as it might just be seen as a fancier Taco Bell, which is part of Yum!

Brands Inc. (YUM), if it doesn't maintain its former image.

For this area, I tend to like Elon Musk's Tesla Inc. (TSLA) the best because he is such a visionary. His types of companies include electric vehicles, SpaceX and Mars colonization, his Hyperloop transportation technology, solar panels, and lithium ion batteries. While a lot of these companies offer a lot of promise, other more viable options can pop up at any time taking a giant bite out of what you originally thought was a great idea. Think for example of a company being formed focusing on colonizing the moon instead of Mars, or a new transportation system that is more cost efficient than the Hyperloop that doesn't have the regulatory and legal issues that a Hyperloop might have. If I do decide to start a longer-term speculative position in Tesla, it will be with smaller buys spread over months or even years. This way I can build a position over time instead of doing a big purchase right when the market decides to start treating the company as just another automotive company instead of a fast growth technology company.

Speculative	Market Cap	P/E	Forward P/E	PEG	Dividend Yield
Sears	$43M	NA	NA	NA	NA
Tesla	$51B	NA	NA	NA	NA
Under Armour	$4.0B	NA	79.62	NA	NA
Chipotle	$12B	65.22	51.56	2.40	NA

Table by Trent Welsh

Chapter 14
The Energy Sector

Money Is Not Happiness, Do What You Love Regardless Of The Reward.
- Author

"As Long As You're Going To Be Thinking Anyway, Think Big."
- Donald Trump

The Energy Sector is an important sector as global consumer demand waxes and wanes and new technologies make cleaner energy solutions continually more viable, especially with government subsidies. This sector should encompass about 6% of your portfolio and has a broad variety of options to choose from based on if you prefer big oil company plays, oil service companies, or smaller pure niche plays along with the ever evolving clean energy companies, which continue to make progress in entering new markets and bringing down costs.

Unfortunately though many clean energy companies are in other sectors of the market at this time including in the Technology Sector, the Industrials Sector, and the Utilities Sector. So I try to grab some clean energy exposure in other sectors and concentrate my holdings in the actual energy sector on the oil giants and more regional specialty plays. Although clean energy still has a long ways to go until it is major a market force, perhaps one day deserving its own sector, it is definitely a good idea to find ways to add some clean energy exposure to your portfolio over time as the technology continues to develop while costs decline and storage options continue to evolve.

The ETF for this section of the market is the XLE and is stuffed full of traditional big oil company plays. Many of these companies have performed well over the years and feature attractive dividends as fossil fuels continue to drive the global economy even with the rise of renewables. The XLE is a great simple way to play the ups and downs of oil prices as U.S. based West Texas Intermediate (WTI) becomes more of a global player along with the more traditional global supply based in Brent oil from the North Sea.

I always try to keep an eye on oil over the years as cycles where oil bottoms at around $20-$40 a barrel seem to point towards good opportunities to overweight my portfolio in energy, whereas when oil tries to reach past $80 a barrel, I look for ways to start taking profits in the energy names as I aim to try to keep my position in the sector to 10% or less. If oil approaches $100 or more again usually there are some global dramas happening abroad that are helping to drive oil prices increasingly up. At that point I try to trade more actively in and out of the space for quick profits while trying to keep a keen eye on global oil supplies as a lot of times, when prices reach up this high, a huge glut in oil is often coming over the next year or two as the global drama deteriorates and a ton of new oil starts to hit the market.

A recent development over the past handful of years has been the rapid growth of American energy as a dominant player in the global market as oil fracing has helped the U.S. shed its dependence on foreign oil. Technology advances have allowed the U.S. to produce some of the lowest cost oil and natural gas in the world, especially after the latest oil crash of 2014, where costs had to be driven out of production for oil companies to survive oil when it bottomed out around the $20-$40 dollar a barrel level.

Fossil fuels should continue to fuel the future over the next decade or two and often feature attractive dividends. However, clean energy initiatives continue to attract investor attention as solar panels, wind farms, and other forms of renewable energy continue to evolve as costs come down and production and storage options continue to get more efficient. My position in almost all cases is always to pursue diversity, and not put all of my eggs into one basket. I would recommend most of your actual energy sector holdings in traditional oil companies and services with maybe a smaller speculative position or two in a solar or battery storage company in another sector like the Technology Sector. I personally aim to get a lot of my clean energy exposure from other sectors of the market such as a Tesla (TSLA) stock in the Consumer Discretionary Sector, known for its electric cars, solar panels, and lithium batteries, or a General Electric (GE) stock in the Industrials Sector, which has put billions into broad based clean energy initiatives in the past, although it has yet to see much in the way of profits from the investments so far.

After your core XLE or mutual fund position is initially set up for a base, I personally looked for a big dividend oil company paired with a major service company for my twin main holdings in the sector. Big dividends and good potential growth are keys for the area along with dominance in a particular area of the world. Notice that global juggernauts like Exxon Mobil Corporation (XOM) and Chevron Corporation (CVX) have exposure to just about every market out there and feature holdings in upstream along with downstream services. Compare this with services companies like Haliburton Company (HAL), which has greater North American exposure compared to a more global services play like Schlumberger Limited (SLB). Figure out what range of dividends you are looking for, and the expected growth of each similar company, and then determine if you want to lean more towards a global or regional specialty company and go from there.

Also note that this sector is an excellent way to gain International exposure in your portfolio by taking energy bets in other parts of the world that are global leaders in their respective markets. I have traded in PJSC Gazprom (OGZPY) as a Russian natural gas play and might consider the upcoming Saudi Aramco IPO if its shares eventually get listed on a U.S. market in the coming years. Also don't forget long-shot deep-water drilling companies like Transocean Limited (RIG) that operates out of Switzerland, especially if oil heads towards $80 and above, as a more speculative play on rising oil prices.

Here are some of the main energy plays I have considered and traded over the years to play in the energy space including Exxon Mobile (XOM), Chevron

(CVX), Schlumberger (SLB), Haliburton (HAL), and Russia's Gazprom (OGZPY).

Energy	Market Cap	P/E	Forward P/E	PEG	Dividend Yield
Exxon	$291B	16.96	14.76	0.77	4.78%
Chevron	$208B	17.07	13.32	0.40	4.13%
SLB	$52B	NA	22.84	NA	5.32%
Haliburton	$24B	24.93	14.61	0.74	2.65%
Gazprom	$50B	3.01	2.52	0.26	5.27%

Table by Trent Welsh

As far as value plays go for the sector, some that investors might consider are energy companies that have had trouble in the recent past, but for the most part, have recovered from the damage and are heading back into growth mode. You can also take a look at some MLP's in the sector, which tend to go in and out of favor in the market place pretty quickly as oil prices and supply and demand fluctuate.

Some value plays I have considered trading in the past have been BP p.l.c (BP), Oasis Midstream Partners LP (OMP) which IPO'd in late 2017, and Magellan Midstream Partners LP (MMP). A lot of the

MLP plays are distribution plays with unique tax advantages built into their structures and returning earnings to shareholders as one of their main goals. I like to trade in and out of MLP's rather than looking at owning them for the long-term as they can see substantial upside and downside depending on oil prices, construction concerns, as well as the incoming supply situation. However, their distribution returns can be an awesome value for investors over the short-term, but be ready to head for the hills if sentiment starts to crash for the group. BP just had some issues a few years ago, which brought it to its knees, but it has recovered nicely and still trades at a discount to many of the other majors out there making it more of a value play at this time in my mind.

Value	Market Cap	P/E	Forward P/E	PEG	Dividend Yield
BP	$131B	13.48	10.68	0.43	6.34%
Magellan	$13B	10.34	11.17	1.29	6.87%
Oasis	$479M	10.66	9.42	0.19	9.89%

Table by Trent Welsh

For speculative plays in the space, a lot of times I consider energy pure plays in a particular area of the market during a specific time in history. Consider deepwater oil plays like Transocean (RIG), or Permian Basin energy companies like Concho Resources (CXO) and Diamondback Energy (FANG). These stocks are nice plays to trade around a few years at a time if oil is on the rise, but are easily droppable when oil prices start to crash or maybe production starts to move away from areas like the Permian Basin over time. These stocks can do remarkably well in the right circumstances, but can take years to recover a quick plunge in oil prices.

Speculative	Market Cap	P/E	Forward P/E	PEG	Dividend Yield
Transocean	$3.3B	NA	NA	NA	NA
Concho	$21B	30.09	21.65	0.40	NA
Diamondback	$10B	13.22	14.17	0.40	0.52%

Table by Trent Welsh

The Energy Sector is a sector that might see big changes in the future as renewables eventually overcome fossil fuels in the coming decades, which means that this whole sector might gradually disappear over time. The alternative is that fossil fuel exposure shrinks in this sector, until more established renewable energy companies are brought in to shore it up, as investors over the coming decades switch to more renewable energies. It is always hard to predict the future, but the U.S. at least seems to be heading quickly to more sustainable energy even with the expansion of the Permian and other basins. However, the effects might not be fully seen and felt by the majority of investors for another decade or two.

Right now most renewable energy stock plays are in other sectors, which means that I like to grab small doses of them in other sectors that add up to some decent holdings as a whole though they do not form a majority of any other sector. Feel free to change how you allocate your resources across different sectors right now in regards to how much renewable energy exposure you want, but you should still have at least 5%-10% of your portfolio based around the fossil fuel market, and its services, in your portfolio means global growth is still reliant on them for the foreseeable future.

Chapter 15
The Consumer Staples Sector

Think Big, Live Simply, Give Back For All That You Have Received.
- Author

"No One Can Make You Feel Inferior Without Your Consent."
- Eleanor Roosevelt

The Consumer Staples Sector is usually a more defensive sector of the market that should make up about 6% of your portfolio while you are young, and possibly grow into a bigger position, as you get closer to retirement. My current plan, as I age, is to most likely increase my holdings in this sector, and sectors like the Utilities, instead of going overboard on bonds like most money managers would steer you towards especially in the past. Of course, with retirement 20-30 years away, a lot can happen to bond rates in a rising interest rate environment. My philosophy can easily change over the coming years or decades, especially if bond rates head above 4% - 5% yields on AAA rated bonds and the like.

Investors can find some very attractive dividends in this sector, with only a little bit of digging, although growth stories can be a little bit harder to find. With growth a little bit harder lately for companies in this sector, more than a few of them are looking at M&A options for growth instead of trying to grow it organically from within the company.

This sector includes the traditional domestic and international food stocks that most investors are familiar with along with beverage companies, personal household goods companies, and sin stocks like tobacco and alcohol. This sector features more than a few slower growth companies, many with very attractive dividends, which have been around for decades with annual dividend increases. It also has some newer and faster growing companies in the sector, think natural and organic, that can help add some growth, without potential dividend support, if that is what you are looking for in the sector.

After setting up some core holdings in index and mutual funds, investors might want to keep it simple in the sector by owning the Consumer Stables sector ETF, the (XLP) for example while you load up on individual stocks in other sectors like technology first. However, I started out more as a conservative investor so I didn't use the XLP much as General Mills (GIS) was one of the first individual stocks I owned as a beginning investor. I have always been a fan of good dividend stocks that trade at a good value in the market, which I like to invest in for the long-term especially when they have predictable annual dividend increases.

With only about 5% of your portfolio dedicated to this sector of the market, that would mean usually one or possibly two big name core holdings to focus your investments on in my opinion along with one value or speculative stock to round out the sector initially. Here are some of my favorite plays in the sector over the years that are worth looking at including The Proctor & Gamble Company (PG), Mondelez International Inc. (MDLZ), PepsiCo Inc. (PEP), Unilever plc (UL), and The Coca-Cola Company (KO).

Consumer Staples	Market Cap	P/E	Forward P/E	PEG	Dividend Yield
PG	$226B	22.36	20.54	3.40	3.17%
Mondelez	$58B	17.93	16.39	2.22	2.62%
PepsiCo	$153B	18.68	19.12	2.69	3.43%
Unilever	$61B	23.35	19.63	4.03	3.52%
Coca-Cola	$199B	29.81	22.38	4.44	3.34%

Table by Trent Welsh

    This is a great sector to take a look at Dividend Aristocrats and Dividend Kings, companies that feature a rising dividend value proposition to shareholders, instead of focusing on rapid growth or speculative M&A activity. For example, Proctor and Gamble (PG) has paid a dividend every year since its inception in 1890! A pretty amazing story over the last 127 years, and it is also expected to increase its annual dividend for the 62nd year in a row in 2018. This is truly a remarkable accomplishment in today's world, and I have no problem owning a few of these types of companies in my portfolio to help balance out my growth and speculation bets.

    I have always been a big fan of diversity in my portfolio and in life, and I look forward to adding to positions in companies like Proctor and Gamble over the years. The closer I get closer to retirement as they potentially become larger percentage holdings in my portfolio. I even kept shares of Proctor and Gamble instead of trading them in for shares of Coty Inc. (COTY) when that company merged with Proctor and Gamble's beauty brands in 2015. No reason to get cute with a century long winner. Just put some money in every half a dozen years and let it ride for decades while collecting the dividend.

    As far as value plays in the sector, I like to look at some out of favor stocks in the sector that are having a difficult time keeping up with the changes in consumer tastes, and that have to turn to acquisitions to find growth and diversification to their brands. Also worth looking at are beaten down stocks like the tobacco companies, which a huge part of the market shuns on principle alone, allowing them to potentially trade at times at great values while sporting very attractive dividends. Tobacco stocks are not for a lot of investors, nor have I ever traded them, but I don't blame people for holding their stocks as the dividends are often very enticing and the stocks pretty stable after the industry consolidated when they went out of favor. Here are some of the stocks to maybe take a look at for a value play including General Mills Inc. (GIS), Philip Morris International Inc. (PM), The Clorox Company (CLX) and The Kraft Heinz Company (KHC).

Values	Market Cap	P/E	Forward P/E	PEG	Dividend Yield
General Mills	$23B	15.41	12.72	2.55	5.02%
Philip Morris	$103B	12.47	13.22	1.62	6.86%
Clorox	$19B	26.23	24.13	4.76	2.53%
Kraft Heinz	$53B	15.35	11.99	2.43	5.77%

Table by Trent Welsh

General Mills (GIS) is an interesting case as cereals and gluten are some of the latest foods to fall out of favor over the last decade, in a transition to natural and organic foods and yogurts, instead of carbs based foods. The funny thing here is that General Mills is also a big seller of yogurts as well as it owns the Yoplait brand. However, it failed to seize an opportunity to develop natural and organic Yoplait varieties before competition did, leaving it behind the 8-ball in places where it could have been a potential leader. It is more of a traditional player struggling to find growth and innovation of any type within its own brands, and thus, it has to turn to acquisitions like its latest Blue Buffalo (BBLFO) purchase in the fast growing pet sector. I believe acquisitions like this will help General Mills in the long-term, but it might take a year or two to be reflected in the stock price, as many feel that General Mills had to over pay for that growth.

As far as speculation plays go in the Consumer Staples sector, I look for some of the small, fast-growing "natural and organic" plays personally. These companies might not have a ton of sales yet, but they might be interesting and trendy plays, with potential special growth and acquisition qualities about them, that might make them a target of larger dinosaurs like General Mills that are desperate for growth. Also some of the companies in a trendy drinks category like craft beers and alcohols that are ultra fast growing might be good and tradable names, or might even be worth a long-term bet if you feel like they have staying power.

I might have one or at most two of these in my portfolio at any given time, but usually I am in these for the short term if I think a catalyst might be on the horizon such as a possible buyout announcement that coincides with a nice potential earnings surprise. These plays are easy for me to sell though once I have made some money in them as I would rather play the speculation growth plays in other sectors usually more than this sector. However, here are a few names in this sector I have traded in the past, or which I have considered putting money down on especially when M&A in the sector starts to heat up. They include Monster Beverage Corp. (MNST), The Hain Celestial Group (HAIN), Campbell Soup Company (CPB), and Sprouts Farmers Market Inc. (SFM).

Speculation	Market Cap	P/E	Forward P/E	PEG	Dividend Yield
Monster	$27B	27.36	27.17	1.64	NA
Hain Celestial	$1.7B	76.08	14.38	20.62	NA
Campbell Soup	$10B	185	13.31	NA	4.29%
Sprouts Farmers Market	$3B	18.73	18.60	1.34	NA

Table by Trent Welsh

A lot of these smaller food and beverage companies make attractive acquisition targets for bigger companies along with nice growth and performance in their own little niches. However, especially when M&A activity in the space heats up, a lot of these names can trade at enhanced valuations for that speculation along with growth multiples that regular food stocks could only wish they had in the sector. With about half a dozen clear targets marked clearly by analysts as potential take-outs at any given time, I don't mind having a small position in one or two of these that I trade in and out of as M&A activity ebbs and flows.

Monster Beverage Case

Monster Beverage Corp. (MNST) is an especially interesting name in the group, which I have profitably traded in and out of over the past few years as it continues to grow nicely across the world. Monster has been buoyed by a strategic partnership with The Coca-Cola Bottling Company Consolidated (COKE), which is The Coca-Cola's (KO) global distribution network. Not only do Monster and Coke have a major strategic partnership, Coca-Cola bought directly into Monster when it bought a 16.7% stake in the company in 2014 for a cool $2.15 billion.

It seems like just a matter of time before Coca-Cola potentially finishes what it started and ends up buying the rest of Monster in my opinion. This is especially true after the summer of 2018, when I believe some of the restrictions from its first Monster acquisition loosen up for Coke, in finding a way to get more or the entirety of Monster. I am a big fan of speculation bets like this when I think the underlying company is doing a great job with their business model as well which Monster appears to be doing with its global expansion. A stock like this though I easily trade into and out of small positions if it makes a nice run or if another stock comes up that I really want a a few shares of. I might hit or miss a potential takeover from Coke, but I'm also fine with taking profits and making bets now on what I think has a good chance to really move while moving into and out of Monster.

At the end of the day however, the question always is, how long should investors wait for a potential acquisition to happen, and can your money be doing better for you in another investment over that time period. Finally, I have had some very nice gains in Monster in the past from performance, along with Coke acquisition speculation, and it just felt like it was the right time to take some profits off the table. This has proven to be a great idea in the past as Monster is not immune from nice bear runs as carbonated beverages continue to struggle across the globe although the energy drink market continues to perform better in this segment then traditional players.

Chapter 16
The Industrials Sector

Don't Be Afraid To Follow, Don't Be Afraid To Lead, Don't Be Afraid To Be Who You Truly Are.
- Author

"A Prophet Is Not Without Honor Except In His Own Country."
- Jesus From Mark 6:4-6

    The Industrials Sector of the market is a potentially booming part of the economy in future years as America's infrastructure, including its roads and bridges, are wearing out across the United States. Both political parties seem open to wanting to find a way to address the problem, though of course each wants the opportunity to be at the center of the $100's of billions or trillions of dollars in spending that is needed.

    Bi-partisan potential support and the deteriorating infrastructure conditions across the country lead me to want to have at least 6% of my portfolio in this sector. I have been a little bit light in this sector in the past and I have been trying recently to increase my exposure to the sector especially at the starts of new years when I try to do some rebalancing.

I'm always trying to determine which sectors to overweight for the following years, besides continued general diversification, and industrials seem a potentially nice place to be if the U.S focuses on an infrastructure bill before or during the next election cycle.

The basic sector ETF for the Industrials is the XLI and includes a diverse set of subsectors such as construction and engineering, heavy equipment companies, the airlines and railroads, and aerospace and defense. This is quite a lineup of different companies spread out in this sector doing lots of varied activities meaning that investors should have little trouble in finding potentially winning companies to make bets on within one or more of these different subsectors.

With infrastructure a potential politically key issue over the next few years, as well as potentially for decades if big bills are decided on, construction and engineering firms have been one of my focuses and core holdings in this sector in the recent past. Railroads and airlines seem to follow major cycles of doing well for a few years, followed by cycles of overly poor performance, so I try to take closer looks at those when

I think they start looking like value plays after bottoming out for a couple of years.

Under political administrations like the Trump administration, bets on aerospace and defense could have the potential for outperformance as he is intent on beefing up the military again. This is similar to betting on health care facilities and providers during the previous Obama administration, as health care reform was a main area of his focus during his presidential administration. When Trump comes up on his re-election campaign though, look for defense stocks to maybe start to slow down, or even underperform, as investors rotate out of them into other areas of the market as a new president would be unlikely to be as bullish on defense as Trump seems to be. Don't ever be afraid to take profits, especially when uncertainty starts to enter into the equation.

After my main mutual funds were set up, I concentrated on some of the bigger sectors first before slowly expanding out into these smaller sector plays. With these smaller sectors a lot of times it is nice to do some research on stocks in there first, or talking with an advisor or friends who are into stocks, for some beginning targets. In my case, my first core position in the space was an engineering and construction company named Jacobs Engineering Group Inc. (JEC). Not many investors have heard of this company, which was recommended to me by my Edward Jones advisor. However, it has performed admirably over the past few years as a low debt company, that recently added some debt to purchase privately held CH2M. This transaction already seems to be paying handsome dividends for the company as Jacobs's margins and revenues are already improving as it finishes up the integration before focusing on reducing its debt to more traditional levels again after 2018. I have maintained this small company as my original core position in the sector, while slowly trying to add larger market cap companies into my portfolio over time, working my way into this sector differently than from the standard top to bottom approach based on my Edward Jones's advisor.

    Here are some of the larger names in the sector that I like, which I have traded into and out of when opportunities arise. However, I have not really invested a lot of money into the lead companies so far in this sector yet as I started with smaller names and value names and plan on adding the biggest names last. This sector has been one of my biggest laggards, and I have been working to catch it up to my goals with some investments over the course of this year and a likely probable heavy IRA investment over the next year or two to help shore it up with some of the biggest names. Here's some of the bigger cap companies I am looking at buying into including Caterpillar Inc. (CAT), The Boeing Company (BA), Lockheed Martin (LMT), Honeywell International Inc. (HON), and 3M Company (MMM).

Industrials	Market Cap	P/E	Forward P/E	PEG	Dividend Yield
Caterpillar	$72B	11.86	10.44	0.54	2.83%
Boeing	$177B	20.20	20.57	0.88	2.64%
Lockheed Martin	$73B	14.99	14.68	0.33	3.41%
Honeywell	$96B	22.84	16.28	3.43	2.52%
3M	$107B	20.23	18.45	2.25	2.96%

Table by Trent Welsh

One of the biggest problems I have had in establishing a core position in these bigger names is because of the big run a lot of them have had over the past couple of years, where Caterpillar (CAT) and Boeing (BA) in particular have had remarkable runs, making it hard for me to find an attractive entry point. With global trade worries and tariff issues seeming around every bend, I am hoping a good entry point appears when I have some cash sitting around to toss into most likely a Caterpillar (CAT) or Boeing (BA) for a core large market cap position. If my timing continues to be off, I will most likely put one or both of them into my IRA next year, which I initially wouldn't plan on touching until retirement.

Most of my work in this sector in the past has been more on the value side of the sector, with investments in nicely growing and super safe historically low debt Jacobs Engineering (JEC). I have been more than happy to own this company for the past few years as it continues to perform admirably each and every quarter, and has promising upside after its recent CH2M acquisition.

Here are some value plays in the industry that I think are currently potentially attractive: Canadian National Railway Company (CNI), Alaska Air Group Inc. (ALK), and, of course, Jacobs Engineering (JEC).

Value	Market Cap	P/E	Forward P/E	PEG	Dividend Yield
Canadian National	$53B	9.73	18.00	0.81	1.86%
Alaska Air	$7B	14.18	13.34	1.81	2.20%
Jacobs Engineering	$8B	19.22	10.97	1.59	1.05%

Table by Trent Welsh

As far as speculative stocks in the sector, one that I have started a position in recently is General Electric Company (GE) after its fall from grace, with its stock dropping ever closer to the single digits. This falling knife will be very difficult to predict where it ultimately lands at, as it has already hit several false bottoms. However, I think there is great potential value in its assets and has a clear but difficult path to a recovery that might take years to realize. I started out with a small position in the company with the plan to evaluate further investments in the company every 3-6 months depending on how things are going. The plan is to gradually build a position in the stock over the next year or two as turning around a giant company like this will take lots of time and effort. However, I think it has plenty of great assets and will be successful in a turnaround effort in plenty of time for my retirement. Thus, taking my time will allow me to gradually build a position with small bets along the way that won't impact my near term trading much. This should result in a nice position for me in the company over the next couple of years, as GE's new CEO gets its company sorted out, while the dividend continues to be decent even after cut after the company chopped it in half.

With my goals of establishing a better big core position in this sector along with gradually building a stake in General Electric (GE), I am not focusing on other industrial speculative possibilities as much right now except for possibly quick trades if something pops up on my radar. Here are a couple other small stocks that fit the speculative mold in the sector, which I have looked at and traded in the past including Chicago Rivet & Machine Company (CVR) and EVI Industries, Inc. (EVI).

Speculative	Market Cap	P/E	Forward P/E	PEG	Dividend Yield
GE	$70B	NA	11.41	NA	NA
Chicago Rivet	$31M	15.23	NA	NA	2.62%
EVI	$400M	97.16	NA	NA	NA

Table by Trent Welsh

If I trade in and out of small stocks like these its usually because I see an upcoming catalyst that is appealing with usually a trade out of the position after the catalyst whether it moved the stock up or not. I keep my trades small with a short-term price target that is easy to trade out of once the event happens and the company goes back into obscurity for most investors.

Chapter 17
The Utilities Sector

Greatness Is All Around You, Recognize And Encourage It.
- Author

"Hitch Your Wagon To A Star."
- Ralph Waldo Emerson

      The Utilities Sector is primarily a defensive part of the market known for limited growth and steady dividends for many of its occupants. Because of the high barriers to entry for a lot of these types of businesses, along with plenty of regulations and government scrutiny, there is typically less risk associated with these types of stocks than the typical stock in many other sectors. I recommend adding to this sector after your initial index and mutual funds are set up, and after you have addressed almost all of your other sectors first, unless you feel strongly that a down or bear market is on the near horizon, or if you believe that interest rates will be headed down over the next few years as stocks in this sector can be very rate sensitive. This sector I try to maintain at around 5% of my portfolio at most with a gradual growing over time to a bigger position as I near retirement.

I used the Spider ETF for the Utilities sector (XLU) more than most other Spider ETF's because I spend a lot of my time looking at other more growth orientated sectors of the market. Hence, when I first began building my portfolio, I didn't want to spend a lot of time looking at slow growth companies when there is so much growth that can often be found in other parts of the market. I bought into the XLU for the first time after the market had marvelous returns over 2017. I figured that it was time to add to my more defensive positions for the start of 2018 with a bunch of my IRA money for that year and noticed that my Utilities exposure now lagged with after the nice gains the rest of my portfolio had in 2017.

The XLU should be able to withstand a lot of the volatility of 2018, including concerns over tariff wars and a potential global slowdown, much better than most of my regular stocks, while still collecting a nice dividend that is approximately twice that of the S&P 500 index fund that I prefer to trade, the (SPY). With the (SPY) paying out about a 1.75% dividend and the XLU receiving about a 3.5% dividend at the beginning of 2018, there is nothing wrong with having some exposure to some nice dividends as long as it doesn't become too big a part of your portfolio as you build it over time. Have some growth and have some dividends, but stay balanced in your long-term goals especially as they change over time.

As I have finished rounding out my portfolio, my last sector to get a single stock purchase was the Utilities sector with a purchase of Dominion Energy Inc. (D). My initial investment in Dominion Energy was a small interest in my portfolio as I already have the XLU and mutual funds for most of the 5% exposure I am aiming for. I plan on making small investments in Dominion, or maybe one of the other core names in the sector, over the next quarter or two to build up a regular position over the back half of 2018.

Some of the main divisions in the Utilities Sector are utilities that provide electricity, water, and gas services along with some hybrids that have several lines of businesses. A lot of the utility companies out there service a local geographical area, so maybe you want to invest in a local provider compared to focusing on dividends or a utility that has more growth than other comparable utilities. Here are some I have looked at briefly in the past as I plan to focus on some of the bigger names in the sector over time including Duke

Energy Corporation (DUK), Dominion Energy Inc. (D), NextEra Energy Inc. (NEE), and Sempra Energy (SRE).

Utilities	Market Cap	P/E	Forward P/E	PEG	Dividend Yield
Duke	$60B	21.39	17.81	4.85	4.38%
Dominion	$47B	20.35	17.34	2.94	4.71%
NextEra	$81B	13.24	21.81	1.72	2.62%
Sempra	$29B	63.66	19.70	7.41	3.34%

Table by Trent Welsh

Some of the value plays in the industry are maybe utility players that might have some growth coming in the future that might let them be a better value today than they will be in the future. Some I am looking at now for possible future investments include CenterPoint Energy Inc. (CNP), MYR Group Inc. (MYRG), and El Paso Electric Company (EE).

Value	Market Cap	P/E	Forward P/E	PEG	Dividend Yield
CenterPoint	$14B	28.73	17.78	3.24	4.08%
MYR Group	$464M	17.72	16.01	NA	NA
El Paso	$2B	18.64	19.91	3.66	2.97%

Table by Trent Welsh

    I have traded some utilities briefly at times in the past when I mostly needed a placeholder stock. I would buy a utility stock or the XLU for a short period of time, or if a dividend was coming up and the timing seemed ok, while I waited for another stock to hit a trading range that interested me more.

    As far as speculative stocks go in this sector the main name that comes to mind is the California utility company PG&E Corp. (PCG). The Pacific Gas and Electric Company covers about 2/3rds of California and is headquartered in San Francisco. First off, this company is subject to more regulations and environmental concerns than most other utility companies because of the fact that it is located in California. It also got blamed, in late 2017, for the start of a massive California wildfire that resulted in the company canceling its dividend as potential liability results come in over the next couple of years. This also has resulted in the stock taking a nice dive of almost 40% from its recent highs, near the end of 2017, before the wildfire struck.

    This means that it might be trading at an incredible value right now, although it is always very hard to say where the bottom is especially when litigation in California is the main concern. It is also a big concern on how many years the company will have to function without a dividend as well. Hence, why it is one of the biggest speculative stocks in the sector at this time. I have learned to try to be more patient with these types of stocks though and not just jump right in after a quality company takes a 40% nosedive. Sometimes I am patient and sometimes I move too soon, but I am always trying to learn and better time when I initiate positions in these types of stocks. In the case of California's PG&E company I am choosing to stay on the sidelines at least until 2019 to see how things play out, especially with the litigation and how it evolves. With a big overhang and that will overshadow any potential catalysts, I wouldn't be surprised if PG&E was dead money for the rest of 2018 and most of 2019 as litigation might take years to sort out.

Speculative	Market Cap	P/E	Forward P/E	PEG	Dividend Yield
PG&E	$12B	43.76	6.27	11.10	NA

Table by Trent Welsh

Chapter 18
The Real Estate Sector

Life Is Far Too Short Not To Take A Big Risk Now And Then.
- Author

"A Real Entrepreneur Is Somebody Who Has No Safety Net Underneath Them."
- Henry Kravis

    The Real Estate Sector was originally part of the Financial Sector, but then split off from it in late 2016 into its own GICS classification. Thus the Real Estate Spider ETF the XLRE was born. I try to keep my exposure to this sector on the low side of about 3% now means I have invested in physical real estate by owning my own home, which is a major long-term investment. This means that I want only minimal exposure to real estate in my stock portfolio, with most of that being centered on the more commercial aspects of Real Estate, instead of more residential real estate when I already own my own home.

    Investors who rent an apartment might be inclined to have considerably more exposure to real estate in their portfolio. I would aim more for 5%-8%

of your portfolio, split mainly between commercial and residential, while reducing some other sectors accordingly. Then, if an investor decides to purchase physical real estate either for a home or business, I would recommend lowering your portfolio exposure down to around 2% again.

Many investors look to Real Estate Investment Trusts (REITS) for their exposure in this sector of the market. This means that REIT investors hold shares in a trust that owns and manages a collection of real estate properties or mortgages on behalf of shareholders. This gives investors a diverse and large range of potential investment possibilities because you can buy stocks in an individual REIT based with ownership based on specific locations like New York or California, or a sector like telecommunications properties for cell phone towers, or even a REIT focused on properties for up and coming data centers for technology players. You can have REITs focused on mall properties, hospitals, or general health care facilities.

What makes REITs appealing to many investors is that they have strict guidelines, that most other companies do not have, that include at least 90% of taxable income must be distributed in dividends back to investors. This is one reason why the closer you get to retirement, the more you might want to expand your portfolio exposure to these types of assets for income production.

A lot of older investors, who don't mind a little risk, love investing in high dividend REITs for some of their income needs. Of course, there is significantly more risk with these instruments than holding treasury bonds, or regular AAA rated bonds for example, as real estate crashes or pullback periodically happen and companies like Amazon.com (AMZN) can help cripple mall REITs, or golf course REITs start to sour when the hype of the sport dies down when a star like Tiger Woods isn't drawing crowds of spectators and golfers to the sport like he did in his glory years.

A lot of stocks in this sector have generous dividends, and so are more susceptible to interest rate risk than other areas of the market. When the Federal Reserve is in a period of raising interest rates over several years, this can put pressure on a lot of REITs, as all of a sudden their riskier 4% dividend doesn't look as attractive when rates treasury rates move past 3% and start heading to 4%, for example. The higher that rates go, the less investors will want to hold on to riskier assets for a little extra dividend potential, instead of safer less risky treasury bonds that hold enough dividends to make investors happy.

    For a core holding in this sector, I look towards some of the bigger commercial players in the industry, which provide a broad exposure to the real estate plays of my choice. I like looking at real estate plays that I think will be a good value and have good growth going forward along with a nice dividend that the company can grow over time. This is another sector that I try to look for dividends in almost every instance and combine that with some future growth prospects. Some of my favorite companies to look at and trade over time in this sector have included American Tower Corporation (AMT), Simon Property Group Inc. (SPG), Equity Residential (EQR), and Ventas Inc. (VTR).

REITs	Market Cap	P/E	Forward P/E	PEG	Dividend Yield
American Tower	$70B	60.38	53.27	8.47	2.13%
Simon Property	$53B	22.27	22.26	2.86	4.85%
Equity Residential	$25B	36.85	38.73	7.16	3.37%
Ventas	$21B	46.43	43.14	NA	5.48%

Table by Trent Welsh

  Some of the best value REITs out there, in my mind, are the ones that have some of the highest dividend yields at the time that I am looking along with being good and stable companies as well. These rates can hit anywhere from 5%-10% for the highest yielders, but be careful you aren't grabbing one that has been sharply heading lower recently because the business is slowly being driven into the ground. Finding some of the best high-yield REITs as times change is an activity I look forward to expanding into as I get older. I hope to do more of this once my core portfolio is fully set up with quality growth stocks and I'm trying to find more and more lucrative and stable dividends hiding in the weeds. Here are some that have especially juicy dividends at this time that I might consider trading in and out of if I need a short term parking place, especially if an ex-dividend date is near. Gaming and Leisure Properties Inc. (GLPI), Kimco Realty Corp. (KIM), New Senior Investment Group Inc. (SNR), and CorEnergy Infrastructure Trust Inc. (CORR).

Value	Market Cap	P/E	Forward P/E	PEG	Dividend Yield
Gaming and Leisure	$7B	17.93	17.47	1.37	8.38%
Kimco	$6B	27.56	14.20	6.11	7.70%
New Senior	$352M	NA	NA	NA	12.12%
CorEnergy	$401M	18.50	17.88	NA	8.93%

Table by Trent Welsh

Speculative plays in the space are those that look like they might have trouble maintaining their current dividend due to a declining or endangered business model, or from a sharp drop in real estate prices in an area for example. A big drop in share price along with an enlarged dividend might be very tempting to many if there is true hope that the business model can be salvaged and the company returned to stability without a cut in the dividend. Some of the suspiciously high dividend players in REITs that currently fit into my speculative model include Wheeler Real Estate Investment Trust Inc. (WHLR) which has recently axed its former massive dividend, Unit Group Inc. (UNIT), and Government Properties Income Trust (GOV).

Speculative	Market Cap	P/E	Forward P/E	PEG	Dividend Yield
Wheeler	$11M	NA	NA	NA	NA
Unit	$2.9B	NA	557.29	NA	14.60%
Government Properties	$1.4B	NA	25.37	NA	24.22%

Table by Trent Welsh

Anything over a 10% dividend yield at this point and time should be looked upon with great concern and skepticism by investors. Most times there is probably a very good reason why lots of institutions and investors aren't crowding heavily into the stock at those yields, ultimately driving up the share price and the yield down to a more normal level. There should be a corresponding associated risk to go along with the enhanced dividend yields, which investors should carefully ponder, analyze, and read an article or two about before stepping in.

I'd of course recommend doing your own good due diligence by reading a conference call or two to get managements thoughts on the current state of the business. Follow this up with a news report or two along with reading a positive and negative article on the stock, if at all possible, from sources such as Seeking Alpha at seekingalpha.com. A lot of times it ends up being a much smarter play to take a tremendous value in a 5%-6% speculative dividend, than playing with fire in a 10% plus dividend, unless you do your homework and are still a believer in the company and are prepared to get out quickly if the going starts gets tough. Even then, I'd suggest playing with a small position in the company for a quarter or two before ramping up to a full position just so that time can help bring out any additional concerns in the company that are not evident after your initial investigation.

Chapter 19
Bonds

Every Moment Of Every Day Is Another Chance To Excel In This Breath That Is Life.
- Author

"Example Is Not The Main Thing In Influencing Others, It Is The Only Thing."
- Albert Schweitzer

Investors should consider some minimum exposure to bonds when they start out their retirement portfolio, just so that you get used to the way they work and how they pay out their coupons for future reference. I'm thinking like 1% of your portfolio or less in a bond mutual fund or a AAA rated bond ETF so that you can see how it performs compared to stocks in your initial mutual funds, or beginning index funds, when the market goes up or down as an investor begins their investing career.

After a small initial stake to learn from at the beginning of your investment career, I wouldn't put much more into bonds until your portfolio reached around $100,000, or if you are close enough to retirement where you actively wanted to allocate a greater and greater portion of your portfolio to income producing assets like bonds. For most of my investing career I currently plan on having bonds being no more than 2%-3% of my total portfolio until maybe the age of 55 or 60 for me personally. Even as I get close to retirement, and into actual retirement, I very well might not have bonds be more than a 10% of my portfolio even at those ages and into my 70's and 80's.

    I have no great desire for a big stake in bonds as I currently would rather focus more on more defensive sectors of the market at those times personally to try to get some growth along with nice dividends. Bonds have their uses, but I have no problem having more defensive positions built into my portfolio in stocks as I age to balance out market crashes, recessions, depressions, and flashes of craziness. Of course, my thesis might change dramatically if bond rates continue to rise over the next decade or two and they make it past 4%-5%. Holding highly rated bonds, bank CDs, and T-bills at 5%+ interest will be a very good case then for a much bigger portion of my portfolio as I get closer to retirement age, but for now I'm fine with a small position in bonds and skepticism that bonds will be heading past 4%-5% in the near future at least.

My initial investment into bonds was as part of a bond mutual fund, that gave me coupons on a monthly basis, which was a great way for me to start getting familiar with how the payments worked for the type of bonds they were along with how they performed over time as the market went up or down compared with my various stock mutual funds.

After I got over the $100,000 mark in my portfolio, I started taking a greater look at the different bond options out there, with funds built of debt from companies set up in a particular ratings level set by Moody's and other debt rating companies. Some of the highest rated bonds are labeled investment grade bonds, and they usually come from stronger companies with strong cash flows along with a moat of security for their business. Of course, these bonds also have corresponding lower yield rates compared to the bonds of riskier businesses and assets, which are rated below investment grade and are more commonly called junk bonds. Junk bonds can be centered around more risky businesses for example, that tend to do great in one climate while not-so-great in another environment like oil companies where the price of oil can jump from $30 a barrel to over $70 a barrel in a year. A lot of bond investing is determining what level of risk you are comfortable with in your bonds to receive the highest coupon rate possible for that level of risk you are willing to bear.

Bonds have a distinct advantage over stocks in that, if a company goes bankrupt, bond holders would usually receive the results of a liquidation long before stock holders would receive a penny according to a judge's ruling. Of course, there is also not as much upside or downside built into bonds and coupons besides the general rise and fall of Fed Rates over time. As rates go up, bonds with higher yields come down in principle price as the yields are not as attractive anymore whereas, when rates go down, higher yielding bonds tend to have their principle amounts go up as they are now more attractive to investors as rates decline elsewhere.

Bonds are interest rate sensitive and the coupon or yield for investment grade bonds a lot of times is approximately 2-3 percentage points higher than current treasury yields. These rates can go up dramatically in businesses that are deemed "risky" by credit rating institutions, and these bonds have the potential to make or lose a lot of money over the short-term if a business increases or decreases its risk profile dramatically like an oil company when oil prices rise or drop rapidly.

When the Fed raises rates making "riskless" treasuries yield more, bond principles of all corporate or municipal bonds tend to drop as their yields become less attractive compared to the base "riskless" treasury case. Similarly, when the Fed lowers rates, bond principles of all shapes and sizes tend to rise in theory, as now their yields are potentially even more enticing compared to the now lower treasury yields.

Bonds are a different type of investment, so when looking at more individual types of bonds a lot of times you should be prepared for minimum requirements for purchases of at least $1,000 in increments of $1,000 if you wanted bonds of Apple (AAPL) for example. There is also not as much liquidity generally associated with individual bonds as there is with stocks although the bond market is a bigger market currently in the U.S. Bonds are a bigger market, but they are not generally traded as much as stocks on most days by individual investors.

At the end of 2017, the total U.S. bond market was over $40 trillion including more than $14 trillion in U.S. Treasury debt, over $9 trillion in mortgage-related bonds, more than $8 trillion in corporate bonds, and almost $4 billion in municipal bonds. Compare this to the U.S. stock market where the Russell 3000, which is about 98% of the market, recently sat at around $30 trillion dollars.

Because the volume on any particular day might be pretty light for a particular bond, make sure that you set up your orders with limits on what you are willing to pay especially if you plan on trading bonds around market news. Most times it is far easier for investors to pick out a bond fund of one type or another that carries bonds of companies similar to what risk level you are looking for. This eliminates a lot of single bond risk and there is generally a lot better liquidity surrounding bond funds compared to individual bonds as well.

Depending on your broker or investing company, you also can try to participate in a corporate or municipal bond offering when they first come to market which can be kind of exciting, like participating in an IPO in the stock world. That way, if your favorite company announces an upcoming offering of bonds, you can try to take part in that offering by contacting your broker or setting up a buy order with purchase info into your trading platform. Bonds are about as exciting as paint drying for many investors out there, but simple things like investing in the bonds of your favorite company for example, can make the experience much more personal and rewarding for an investor, and that much more exciting.

For many investors, the choice of bonds can be simply looking at a table of rates comparing the top bond offerings out at the time and picking the risk/reward scenario that works out best for their risk tolerance. The spread, or the current difference in rates for bonds for different periods of time is one key measure, especially if there is an unusually large or small spread currently built into rates. Here is an example of a simplified table that many investors might use to figure out their bond preferences.

Bonds	3 Mo	1 Yr	3 Yr	10 Yr	30 Yr
U.S. Treasuries	2.3%	2.73%	2.93%	3.14%	3.32%
Corporates (AAA)	NA	NA	NA	NA	NA
Corporates (AA)	NA	2.68%	NA	NA	4.39%
Corporates (A)	1.73%	2.89%	3.32%	4.04%	5.20%
Municipals (AAA)	NA	1.80%	2.26%	3.45%	4.08%
Municipals (AA)	NA	2.65%	2.41%	4.70%	4.51%
Municipals (A)	NA	2.65%	3.21%	4.70%	5.07%

Table by Trent Welsh

Once you have a table in front of you, it's just a matter of whether you want your money locked into shorter or longer periods of rates, the risk level of the bond you are comfortable with, and finally the tax implications, which might cause you to prefer municipal bonds for example. Most times though, I would personally tend to stick with a simple short-term AAA rated Corporate bond fund, as I expect the U.S. to be in a generally slowly rising interest rate environment for the course of the next few years at least.

Chapter 20
Domestic versus International

Consensus Opinion Is A Weakness To Be Exploited.
- Author

"Two Things Are Infinite: The Universe And Human Stupidity;
And I'm Not Sure About The Universe."
- Albert Einstein

    One issue to monitor as you build your portfolio is to have some direct international exposure built into your portfolio from the start to complement U.S. domestic exposure in my case. Most examples in this section are based on the U.S. as the domestic market, but if you are based in another country trading non-U.S. markets, you will of course have to adjust your strategy accordingly. While its true that the economy is a global economy much more so now than even 10-20 years ago, having some stock in companies with headquarters and sales based in other parts of the world should result in greater diversity for your portfolio. Just because Apple (AAPL) sells a lot of iPhones in China doesn't mean that gives you the diversity of owning shares in Alibaba (BABA) for example, which is based in China with most of its sales in China, but its shares can be bought on a U.S. market.

The U.S. has been the best market in the world for long-term growth and earnings over the past 100 years, but many companies like China have put up some great growth numbers now for years along with some other emerging countries having great periodic runs as well. Every country's market will have its ups and downs compared to the rest of the world, along with some direct effects on other parts of the world, especially in the time of crisis or political turmoil. It is nice to have some exposure to some foreign markets that you believe can also outperform in the coming years especially if the U.S. economy decides to take a break for a few years or a decade. Its also a simple way to continue to diversify your growing portfolio so that you have some direct exposure to multiple markets and areas of growth while you take more specific shots on individual companies.

When I first started investing, I first put money into a global growth mutual fund to start out my international holdings right along side domestic growth as well. After I had a solid base built up, I picked up a more specific EuroPacific growth fund for that part of the world. Since then, I have looked at maybe taking a greater shot on China via maybe something like the iShares China Large-Cap ETF (FXI) to complement my main single stock risk based in Alibaba (BABA) stock which I own by proxy through Altaba (AABA) and SoftBank Group (SFTBY). I have also looked at and traded mining companies in Africa, oil and gas companies from the Middle East, Russia, and Latin America, along with additional banking companies from around the world.

Starting out I would think 5%-10% would be a nice place to start for some international exposure with the rest mainly in domestic markets in the U.S for a trader based in U.S. markets. The U.S. continues to be the global business and financial leader, even with the emergence of China, so it's usually best just to start out following the lead dog, especially if you trade on U.S. markets. After you have your base properly set up, and are expanding more into individual stocks, I'd recommend trying to up your allocation more around 80% U.S. and 20% international as a target to aim for over the longer term. Of course, if you are a Chinese trader based in China with knowledge of Chinese companies you might want to have more like 80% Chinese domestic companies and 20% based in countries like the U.S.

As international markets continue to develop and expand, and countries like Saudi Arabia and other emerging markets become more and more investable, I might end up expanding my international exposure more towards 25%-30% of my portfolio. I will figure this out specifically over the next decade or two for me personally especially if the markets and stocks of some emerging markets do a good job on transparency and political stability for a reasonable amount of time.

However, for now I am fine with trying to keep my international exposure between 15%-20% as over the course of the year I tend to invest more in domestic U.S. companies as news and catalysts emerge over the year. One of the main areas I look at when the year ends is my international exposure, as a lot of times this can easily get out of whack buying and selling over the course of the year. This usually results in some rebalancing needed at the end of every year or with some new IRA contributions to begin the next year.

One of the main concerns with international stocks is the fact that many of them trade on foreign exchanges and not on the regular U.S. based NYSE or NASDAQ markets for example. Companies can be listed on one exchange or multiple exchanges if they want to pay the fees and upkeep for two or more different markets. Take Alibaba (BABA) for example. It is a Chinese company that did its initial public offering (IPOs) on the U.S. market, which means that it is subject to U.S. listing laws and should have as a result more transparency and regular information released about its business practices at this time than most other Chinese companies that trade only on the Chinese Shanghai Stock Exchange or the Hong Kong based Hang Seng.

One way to get international exposure is to buy stock in foreign companies that list on U.S. exchanges via trading in American Depository Receipts (ADRs). These are non-U.S. based companies that you can buy and sell on a U.S. based exchange that pay their dividends to ADR shareholders in U.S. dollars. These instruments allow U.S. investors to easily trade shares of non-U.S. companies without the hassles of any cross-border or cross-currency transactions.

Trading in international stocks is a slightly more complicated and confusing endeavor than regular domestic stocks. However, this should be nothing too scary or intimidating for most investors especially if you stay on the major markets with well-known international companies that have a great track record of performance. However, it is just as easy to say forget being overly complicated and just bulk up on the major mutual funds or ETF's that are dedicated to the global exposure that you are most interested in. I continue to trade with my more broadly based ETF's, primarily in the regions that I love the most, along with individual stocks in some of the international companies that I think have the most promise in the coming years.

Chapter 21
Bitcoin and Cryptocurrencies

The Death Of Reading Is The Birth Of Stupidity.
- Author

"The Only True Wisdom Is Knowing That You Know Nothing."
- Socrates

    Bets on Bitcoin, Etherium, or any number of other crypto currencies would be highly speculative and each would have their own pros and cons that would make them uniquely suited to one particular situation. However, with the massive upside some of these "currencies" or "commodities" have seen in the past come with the real possibility that quite a few of them might ultimately head to zero for whatever reason.

    Personally, I'd much rather trade in and out of these positions by using an instrument like the Bitcoin Investment Trust (GBTC) instead of building a wallet to hold coins, trading them on an exchange, and maintaining the lengthy keys for the future with the possibility that if the keys are ever lost there is no possible way to ever recover your coins.

I've also been waiting for some good ETF's to come out that have exposure to a wide range of coins that is actively known and traded on a big market. That way, if the whole coin market crashes you are just out of luck, but if its only one or two types of coins, the ETF can survive and continue on with some value afterward. With coins and assets that can go up 1000% or more in a year, be very aware that a lot of times there are many good reasons out there for it to continue to rise, but also some very good reasons its might be headed the other direction just as fast in the near future.

I see Bitcoins and other cryptocurrencies as basically a gold substitute and thus as one type of value storage. Thus, just like gold, if I jump into a position it is usually a 1/2 or even 1/4th of a position and never has been a greater portion of my portfolio at least up to this time. I also find it incredibly easy to sell out of the position especially if it has a nice sudden run as I'm more than happy to grab some profits with the volatility as its future valuation is far from certain. Any day the coin could easily be up or down 10%-20% on little to no news and just momentum alone, which makes it a very tricky thing to invest in.

I'm a lot bigger believer in the underlying blockchain technology, which is the basis of crytpcurrencies at this time. I believe blockchain technology definitely has long lasting and tangible effects in many areas of business including the shipping of goods as well as financial transactions for starters. Bitcoin and other coins though usually have a more simple and focused use, which can limit their ultimate upside as each coin has one general good use.

Time will tell how good of an investment Bitcoins and cryptocurrencies are, just be aware of the risks and keep your risk in check with what you are ultimately willing to lose if the market for a coin or all coins gets a sudden correction. They are fine for additional diversity, but be sensible about your risk.

Chapter 22
Over-The-Counter Trading

Juxtaposition. Some Stocks Like Words Are Unique And Worth Holding Forever.
- Author

"I'm Selfish, Impatient And A Little Insecure. I Make Mistakes, I Am Out Of Control And At Times Hard To Handle. But If You Can't Handle Me At My Worst, Then You Sure As Hell Don't Deserve Me At My Best."
- Marilyn Monroe

Right now true global trading across all the markets of the world is still a long ways away. Cheap access to international markets is not really feasible for the regular investor at this time like buying a Chinese company on a Chinese exchange for example. However, many foreign companies who don't want to deal with the time, effort, money, regular reporting, and transparency issues that come with being on a major U.S. exchange can instead trade their shares on the over-the-counter (OTC) market, via an American Depositary Recepts (ADR) for example.

OTC trading is between two parties without the direct supervision of an exchange. Major U.S. exchanges work to help facilitate liquidity, transparency, and true up to the second price information which can be lacking when investors head on over to the OTC market. The OTC markets have less regulations and rules so its easier and cheaper for foreign companies to list their stocks on this market.

OTC markets also have many U.S. stocks that can't meet the requirements of the NYSE or NASDAQ markets for reasons such as market cap size, or stock price if it is a "penny stock", or regular transparent reporting. The U.S. Securities and Exchange Commission (SEC) sets up the reporting rules for all exchanges from the big exchanges to the OTC markets down to the pink sheets or "gray market" stocks which require little to no reporting.

Be aware that the farther away you get from the major markets, the greater chance of inherent risk there is associated with the stocks that you are trading. Make sure that you use limit orders at all times and just be aware that there won't be nearly as much reporting and tracking of these stocks compared to regular major market stocks that most investors rely on.

There are plenty of great stocks trade on these markets though so don't be afraid to use them if you want some more direct exposure to international companies that don't want the bother of listing on a major exchange. A lot of times when I use these markets I also try to take smaller positions in a lot of these stocks due to the increased risk from less transparency and liquidity. Just be aware of the differences in the markets and don't let good opportunities pass you by just because a company isn't listen on a major market.

Chapter 23
Multiple Ticker Symbols

Great Companies Are Like Great People, Inspiring From Top To Bottom.
- Author

"Logic Will Get You From A To B. Imagination Will Take You Everywhere."
- Albert Einstein

Have you ever noticed that stocks like Google (GOOGL), (GOOG) have two ticker symbols that trade publicly, which can sometimes make things a little tricky when deciding on how to invest in the company? Google's Class A shares trade under the GOOGL symbol and have defined voting rights for the company along with typically trading at a premium on the market to its other shares. Google has non-trading Class B shares that founders usually end up with like Google's Sergey Brin and Larry Page along with some other company big-wigs. Class B shares have voting rights of 10 Class A votes per share. Finally, Google has Class C publicly traded shares that have no official voting rights tied to them for the company and usually trade at a discount to

Class A shares by about 2%-3% a lot of times. These Class C shares also have covenants built into them to help protect them from differing too much in price from Class A shares. This helps keep the gap between Class A shares and Class B shares small so that GOOG shares don't end up trading at a 10% or 20% discount to GOOGL shares.

    The main question then becomes, if you want to invest in Google shares, which class of shares should you buy? For me, the difference comes in the discount between the class A and class C shares that usually is the defining characteristic for me especially compared to historical averages. If the difference between the two is around 3% or higher I will usually go for the Class C non-voting shares, whereas if it is less than 3% I usually pay up and go for the Class A voting shares. This is mostly personal preference, but I like the idea of getting the notices of shareholder meetings along with the voting cards to be mailed back with my choices for directors along with the half a dozen or so other issues the company has up for vote each time they have their yearly shareholder meeting.

    Notice also that splitting up shares between class A and class B is seen in other industries also, usually with the intent of preserving voting power for the founder(s). In the media business, 21st Century Fox trades under the tickers (FOX) for class C and (FOXA) for class A, while in the apparel industry, Under Armour trades under the tickers (UA) for class C along with (UAA) for class A shares. When a company splits up its tickers like this, the usual path is to double the total number of shares outstanding of the stock. This results in the two new sets of stocks trading at approximately half the original value of the former single ticker, which means the market cap stays approximately the same for the company.

For example, if there are 100 million shares of Class A stock that are trading at $100 a share at the end of the day, the company would create 100 million shares of the Class C stock after hours when the market was closed. When trading resumed the next day after the split, the 100 million Class A shares would theoretically trade at approximately $50 a share and the 100 million Class C shares at approximately $50 a share. Of course, as soon as the stocks start trading again, they will move up or down depending on investors and market conditions along with a natural discount appearing between the shares as more people would theoretically invest in Class A shares over Class C shares until the gap between them created enough value that investors didn't care about the voting rights.

One case where I will almost always choose non-voting shares is in M&A deals like when Comcast (CMCSA) and Disney (DIS) took up a bidding fight for the right to buy most of the assets of Twenty-First Century Fox (FOX) (FOXA). In this case, Fox Class A shares and Class C shares naturally trade with a built in discount, but in an acquisition or merger deal, Class A and C shares will be bought with the winning companies cash and/or shares at the same price regardless of voting rights or not. Because I plan on holding on to my Fox shares until a deal is done regardless of the winner, I bought the Class C shares of Fox so that I can make the most money when the deal finishes.

Chapter 24
Treasuries

Success Does Not Define You, Failure Does Not Define You,
Future Actions Define You.
- Author

"Always."
- Severus Snape

Now, why are yields important? First, as you get closer to retirement, the Fed rate is an important marker, which can be measured by Treasury Bills which are also called Treasuries or T-bills for short. These are the bond rates backed by the full faith and credit of the United States that banks use to borrow money on from the Federal Reserve, or other banks, to maintain their minimum reserve requirements, lets say 2.75% for a 10 year Treasury.

Now, the bank takes that money and lends it out to a homebuyer taking out a 30-year loan at lets say 5%. The difference in rates between what the bank loans money at and the money it borrows from is called the spread. Borrowing and lending money while profiting from a spread is one of the main sources of income for many financial institutions. In this instance, the bank borrows money at 2.75%, and then lends it out at 5%, which means the spread the bank is making on the loan is 2.25% if you ignore factors like sales costs to keep things simple. Borrowing cheap money from source A and lending that same money to source B at higher rates is not rocket science and is how many banks have been making money for thousands of years.

Treasuries should also be important for investors to monitor as they become older because they form the base of what rate an investor can get in a "risk-free" scenario. This is the return that you can receive by buying Treasuries, backed by the full faith and credit of the U.S. government, which can give you the least risky asset on the market, that earns hopefully a positive interest rate, that can hopefully keep an investor up with inflation.

Now, lets say you reach retirement with a $1,000,000 nest egg. The question becomes, do you want to hold the money in cash which receives little to no interest? Do you want to make 2.75% by investing it into 10 year Treasuries? Do you want to make 3.5% on "riskier" triple A-rated corporate bonds? Do you want to be fully or partially invested in the stock market, which might be up or down 5%-30% or more in any given year? These decisions become very important the closer you get to retirement, especially around the time when you expect to stop receiving regular income from a job or some other source of regular funds. If making $27,500 a year in interest is enough money for you to happily live off of, besides your other savings, maybe having most of your eggs in T-bills is the smart move for you if this "riskless" investment will allow you to have a happy retirement.

Figuring out your financial needs in retirement, with a built in cushion, will help you define and adapt your portfolio over time to aim for the return you want to achieve based on the risk you are ultimately willing to take as you age. A nice goal for any investor would be to have a large enough retirement nest egg that could be almost totally invested in "riskless" T-bills that would provide enough interest income to live off of with a cushion without ever diluting the original principle.

Chapter 25
Portfolio Examples

Life Is Worth Living, It Is The Ultimate Gift And Reward.
- Author

"To Live Is The Rarest Thing In The World. Most People Exist,
That Is All."
- Oscar Wilde

Sample Part of Trent's Portfolio Mid 2018

Company	Ticker Symbol	Sector	~ % of Portfolio
Apple	AAPL	Information Technology	2%
IBM	IBM	Information Technology	4%
Altaba	AABA	Information Technology	2%
Citigroup	C	Financial	1%
HSBC	HSBC	Financial	2%
Deutsche Bank	DB	Financial	2%
Eli Lilly	LLY	Health Care	2%
Sarepta Therapeutics	SRPT	Health Care	4%
Valeant	VRX	Health Care	2%

Pharmaceuticals			
Boeing	BA	Industrials	1%
Jacobs Engineering	JEC	Industrials	3%
General Electric	GE	Industrials	3%
Rangold Resources	GOLD	Materials	1%
U.S. Steel	X	Materials	3%
Hi-Crush	HCLP	Materials	4%
Twenty-First Century Fox	FOX	Consumer Discretionary	7%
Ford	F	Consumer Discretionary	1%
Amazon	AMZN	Consumer Discretionary	2%
Royal Dutch Shell	RDS-B	Energy	2%
Haliburton	HAL	Energy	3%
Transocean	RIG	Energy	3%
PepsiCo	PEP	Consumer Staples	3%
General Mills	GIS	Consumer Staples	6%
Monster Beverage	MNST	Consumer Staples	3%
AT&T	T	Telecommunications	4%
Charter Communications	CHTR	Telecommunications	1%
SoftBank	SFTBY	Telecommunications	2%
Dominion	D	Utilities	2%
Utilities Spider	XLU	Utilities	3%
American Tower	AMT	Real Estate	3%

Dividend Based Portfolio

Company	Ticker Symbol	Industry	Yield
Cisco Systems	CSCO	Information Technology	3.12%
Qualcomm	QCOM	Information Technology	4.21%
New York Community Bancorp	NYCB	Financial	5.92%
Metlife	MET	Financial	3.80%
GlaxoSmithKline	GLAXF	Health Care	5.25%
Sanofi	SNY	Health Care	4.27%
Icahn Enterprises	IEP	Industrials	9.04%
General Electric	GE	Industrials	3.51%
Hi-Crush	HCLP	Materials	7.63%
International Paper	IP	Materials	3.58%
Ford	F	Consumer Discretionary	5.52%
Daimier AG	DDAIF	Consumer Discretionary	6.63%
Royal Dutch Shell	RDS-B	Energy	5.23%
Energy Transfer Partners	ETP	Energy	11.73%
General Mills	GIS	Consumer Staples	4.43%
Philip Morris	PM	Consumer Staples	5.54%
AT&T	T	Telecommunications	6.30%

Qwest Corp	CTAA	Telecommunications	7.05%
Dominion Energy	D	Utilities	4.75%
National Grid PLC	NGG	Utilities	8.87%
Ventas	VTS	Real Estate	5.46%
Tanger Factory Outlet	SKT	Real Estate	6.00%

Tables by Trent Welsh

Index of Terms

Arbitrage – The difference between prices of an item in two different markets or during two different expected time periods. For example, if you can buy bread on one side of town for $1 and sell there for $0.95 compared to the other side of town where you can buy bread for $0.75 and sell for $0.70 the difference is a type of arbitrage situation. The astute investor would buy bread for $0.75 on one side of town and take it to the other side of town and sell it for $.95 thus reaping a $0.20 cent arbitrage profit if costs such as time, effort, and storage to get to the other side of town were negligible.

In M&A situations a lot of times something like this will come up after a deal is closed. The deal is set to close a month from now with a stockholder set to receive $1.00 lets say for every share he/she owns. However, instead of waiting for a month, the stockholder can currently sell their shares on the market for $0.97 a share, a 3% discount that can be viewed as a potential arbitrage situation. Of course, when evaluating these situations, investors have to take into consideration the time their money will be "dead money" until the deal closes, transaction fees for selling out early, along with possibilities that the deal might ultimately be scuttled by an outside force (government or regulatory intervention for example) or even an outside bidder coming in at the last minute with a superior offer that might cause the original contract deal to be terminated in favor of a new offer.

Conglomerate – A corporation with a controlling stake in a number of unrelated businesses or smaller companies which conduct their business units independently from the other business divisions while ultimately reporting to the parent company.

Coupon Rate – The annual interest payment that a bondholder receives from a bond's issue date to maturity typically in semi-annual payments. When Fed rates go up, higher rate coupon bond's principles typically go down as investors are willing to pay less for the higher rate bonds when Fed rates go higher. Conversely, when Fed rates drop, bond principles typically go up as the higher bond rate becomes more intriguing to investors who are willing to pay a higher principle for the bonds with a higher coupon rate.

Dead Money – Money in stocks for example that go nowhere for an extended period of time. This happens when no clear catalysts are on the horizon to drive additional shareholder value. Ideally an investor would want to be diversified with stocks in every sector all with clear catalysts coming within the next months or year that would possibly be enough to drive higher valuations. Of course, stocks can still rise and fall with market crashes and pops like a boat rises and falls on ocean waves, but the core fundamentals and prospects of a stock help determine if it has the ability to drive valuations outside of regular market moves and can escape the dreaded "dead money" scenario.

My most dreaded dead money scenario was waiting for MannKind's (MNKD) Afrezza sales to drive future valuation increases which to date has not happened. Sanofi (SNY) couldn't drive sales, MannKind couldn't drive sales, label changes and additional studies couldn't drive sales, TV ads didn't drive sales, so MannKind has nothing much going for it except hoping blindly for sales increases which have not materialized for years now. This is a "dead money" stock because, at this point, it is highly unlikely to expect sales to dramatically pick up out of nowhere, and there are not really any catalysts on the horizon that could significantly drive sales as most avenues have now been explored.

Dividend Aristocrats – S&P 500 companies that have increased dividend payouts for 25 consecutive years or more within any of the 11 sectors of the S&P 500 index. The 53 S&P 500 companies that fit this description as of January 25, 2018 are 1. 3M Company (MMM), 2. AFLAC Inc. (AFL), 3. AbbVie Inc. (ABBV), 4. Abbott Laboratories (ABT), 5. Air Products and Chemicals Inc. (APD), 6. A.O. Smith (AOS), 7. Archer-Daniels-Midland Co (ADM), 8. AT&T (T), 9. Automatic Data Processing (ADP), 10. Becton Dickinson (BDX), 11. Brown-Forman (BF), 12. Cardinal Health Inc. (CAH), 13. Chevron Corp. (CVX), 14. Cincinnati Financial Corp (CINF), 15. Cintas Corp (CTAS), 16. The Clorox Company (CLX), 17. Coca-Cola Co (KO), 18. Colgate-Palmolive (CL), 19. Consolidated Edison Inc (ED), 20. Dover Corp (DOV), 21. Ecolab Inc. (ECL), 22. Emerson Electric (EMR), 23. Exxon Mobil Corp (XOM), 24. Federal Realty Investment Trust (FRT), 25. Franklin Resources (BEN), 26. General Dynamics (GD), 27. Genuine Parts Company (GPC), 28. W.W. Grainger (GWW), 29. Hormel Foods Corp (HRL), 30. Illinois Tool Works (ITW), 31. Johnson & Johnson (JNJ), 32. Kimberly-Clark (KMB), 33. Leggett

& Platt (LEG), 34. Lowe's Companies, Inc. (LOW), 35. McCormick & Company (MKC), 36. McDonald's (MCD), 37. Medtronic (MDT), 38. Nucor (NUE), 39. PPG Industries (PPG), 40. PepsiCo (PEP), 41. Pentair (PNR), 42. Praxair (PX), 43. Procter & Gamble (PG), 44. Roper Technologies (ROP), 45. S&P Global (SPGI), 46. Sherwin-Williams (SHW), 47. Stanley Black & Decker Inc. (SWK), 48. Sysco (SYY), 49. T. Rowe Price (TROW), 50. Target Corporation (TGT), 51. VF Corporation (VFC), 52. Walmart (WMT), and 53. Walgreen Boots Alliance (WBA).

Dividend Kings – S&P 500 companies that have increased their dividend payouts for 50 consecutive years or more within any of the 11 sectors within the S&P 500 index. The 14 S&P 500 companies that fit this description as of January 25, 2018 are 1. 3M Company (MMM), 2. Dover Corp (DOV), 3. Cincinnati Financial Corp (CINF), 4. Coca-Cola Co (KO), 5. Colgate-Palmolive (CL), 6. Emerson Electric (EMR), 7. Federal Realty Investment Trust (FRT), 8. Genuine Parts Company (GPC), 9. Hormel Foods Corp (HRL), 10. Johnson & Johnson (JNJ), 11. Lowe's Companies, Inc. (LOW), 12. Procter & Gamble (PG), 13. Stanley Black & Decker Inc. (SWK), and 14. Target Corporation (TGT).

Dividend Yield – This ratio is the amount of money a company pays out to shareholders in dividends a year relative to the company's share price. Thus, if a company pays out $1 in dividends per year ($0.25 per quarter), and the company's share price currently sits at $10, this would result in a current dividend yield for the investor of 10%. If the market moved the stock price to $8 the next day, the dividend yield of the stock would jump to 12.5% means you would be paying less for the stock that yielded the same dividend ($0.25 per quarter) as the previous day. Similarly, if the stock rose to $12 the next day, the dividend yield would drop to 8.33% means now you would have to pay more for the stock that had the same dividend as the previous day.

Ex-Dividend – This is the first day that a stock trades where investors who buy the stock do not receive the previously announced upcoming dividend. Thus, if a company announces a dividend on June 1st that will be paid on July 31st with an ex-dividend date of July 28th, shareholders on record for June 27th will receive the upcoming dividend. If a shareholder buys the stock of the company on June 28th they will not be entitled to receive the upcoming dividend that will be paid out on July 31st.

Federal Funds Rate – The Federal Funds Rate is the interest rate at which banks and credit unions lend reserve balances to other depository institutions overnight without collateral. Institutions with surplus balances in their accounts can lend those balances to institutions in need of additional cash inflows at these interest rates.

Forward P/E – Same as the P/E ratio except that its earnings part of the ratio is forecasted 12 months ahead, or a full fiscal year ahead, of where the company currently sits on its earnings. This is a useful tool for analyzing how expensive the stock might look a year from now based on expectations that sales will rise or fall dramatically from the current period. It is also useful in evaluating stocks that currently now have no earnings (thus no current P/E value), but plan to have positive earnings a year from now.

GICS reclassification – Standard & Poor's 1999 Global Industry Classification Standard (GICS) meant to establish global standards for categorizing companies into sectors and industries. It originally set up 10 original sectors including Information Technology, Financials, Health Care, Energy, Industrials, Materials,

Consumer Staples, Consumer Discretionary, Telecommunications Services, and Utilities. In 2016, the GICS expanded the original 10 sectors into 11 sectors by taking Real Estate out of Financials and elevating it to its own independent sector. On September 21, 2018, the Telecommunications Services sector will be renamed the Communications Services sector and will include stocks that now are currently in the Consumer Discretionary and Information Technology sectors. Realign and rebalance your portfolio accordingly to adjust for these changes.

Inflation – The increased costs of goods and services in a market over a specified period of time. If inflation goes up by 2% over the course of a year and you are making 2.5% on Treasuries, the interest you are making on your T-bills should be enough to cover the rising costs of goods and services generally across the market. The inverse scenario is deflation where the prices of goods and services decrease over a specified period of time.

IPO – An Initial Public Offering is an offering of a previously private company's shares onto the open market via a sale to institutions and individual retail investors.

Market Capitalization – Refers to the total market value of all of a company's outstanding shares. For example, if a company has 100 million shares outstanding that are trading currently at $2 a share, its market capitalization would be $200 million. Similarly, if a company has 1 billion shares outstanding and its stock is trading at $100 a share, its market capitalization would be $100 billion. Some of the largest public companies currently in the world are trying to make runs at the $1 trillion dollar market capitalization level. Stocks that are currently trading under a market capitalization of $1 billion dollars might require more detailed research as many won't be highly followed or written on by the investment community.

P/E Ratio – A Price to Earnings Ratio. The higher the ratio is, 40 compared to 20 for example, the higher the stock price is compared to a company's earnings. The higher the P/E ratio, the more "expensive" a stock is although this is just one of many inputs to look at. Stocks with huge growth rates, that are popular with investors, and little earnings could have sky high multiples of like 80-100 or higher whereas stocks, out of favor in the market, with good earnings but low growth could have very low P/E ratios of 8-10 or lower. Stocks with no positive earnings (think early stage biotech companies, or technology companies trying to grow instead of make money) will have no calculable P/E ratio.

PEG Ratio – A Price/Earnings to Growth Ratio. This ratio is the company's P/E ratio divided by the company's growth rate over a specified period of time. The higher the growth rate of a company compared to companies with similar P/E values, the smaller the PEG ratio will be. Thus, generally speaking, most companies would love a PEG ratio under 1, but these ratios always need to be taken into context means so many different variables enter into the mix.

Prospectus – Highly detailed and relevant disclosure information on a particular financial security for institutions and investors to look at including financials, directors, holdings, and other material information on the selected financial security.

Transparency – Regular, detailed, clear, concise, timely, and reliable information on companies including risks so that investors can make intelligent investing decisions when making comparisons. The more informed an investor is, the more likely the investor is going to make a smart business decision.

VIX – A volatility index. When not much trading is going on and the market spends a lot of time in a narrow trading range, the volatility tends to bw small and the VIX registers a lower number of around 10 for example. When markets start to fluctuate wildly up and down, in extreme fashion over short periods of time, this can prompt massive trading spikes, which can lead the VIX to surge past the 30's for example.

About The Author

    Trent Welsh was born in Minnesota in 1978 with a love of reading and an independent spirit ready to take on life's challenges. He graduated from the University of Missouri-Columbia with a B.A. in Psychology followed up with an MBA. He has written and published 142 stock articles on the business website SeekingAlpha.com that have garnered over 1 million page views. The rise of retail investing is a promising endeavor for many investors like Trent who want to take their retirement planning into their own hands and succeed where many money managers ultimately fail.

    Trent currently lives in Illinois with his wife and 5 kids and continues to invest and diversify his portfolio of assets for a happy retirement. Never be afraid to take that step toward greatness.

www.ingramcontent.com/pod-product-compliance
Lightning Source LLC
Chambersburg PA
CBHW071528220526
45469CB00003B/685